Life as Parable

Reinterpreting the Religious Life

by *John Manuel Lozano, C.M.F.*

PAULIST PRESS
NEW YORK/MAHWAH

$8.95 mw 1-21-87 (Rev. R.)

Library of Congress Cataloging-in-Publication Data

Lozano, Juan.
    Life as parable.

    Includes bibliographies and index.
    1. Monastic and religious life.   I. Title.
BX2435.L687   1986   255   86-15057
ISBN 0-8091-2825-X (pbk.)

Published by Paulist Press
997 Macarthur Blvd.
Mahwah, N.J. 07430

Printed and bound in the
United States of America

Contents

iii

Foreword

The idea of presenting a systematic view of the religious life—for the second time in barely five years—came as the result of seeing the favorable welcome that was given my earlier study, first published in Italian *(La Sequela di Cristo, Teologia storico-sistematica della Vita Religiosa)* and then in English *(Discipleship: Towards an Understanding of Religious Life)*. In this first overall study, I tried to bring the vision of the religious life back to its evangelical inspiration, and to keep constantly in mind its historical development and its richness, so as to avoid giving an absolute value to categories that have been used to describe it in recent times. This obliged me to do a close exegesis of biblical sources (those which have really influenced the religious life) and to refer back constantly to history.

This very procedure made the book less accessible to those who did not have an adequate academic background. Since the book has been used not only in chapters and in university programs, but also in a number of programs for the initial formation of religious, I thought it convenient to offer the latter a book in which the exposition would be less crowded with technical details and quotations from antiquity. I wanted it to be a serious study, yet one which would flow more easily. It would likewise have to be a more summary treatment.

With this in mind, I set about writing this second study. I soon found, however, that books, like children, look rather different with the passage of time: although they share some common traits, they are never quite identical. Between books, the author has gone on living, experi-

1

menting, studying and reflecting, and new points of view have crept into the creation of this new study. The reader will note some new notions from recent Christology, a more prolonged reflection on Jesus' favorite theme of the kingdom of God, a greater sensitivity to the encounter and sometimes the shock between charism and ecclesiastical institutions, a greater attention to the human problems involved in celibacy, a dialogue with theologies of the religious life developed in the third world, especially in Latin America, etc. The life of the Church during these intervening years, which is a fundamental part of the life that the author has enjoyed and suffered, is reflected throughout this new study.

Even so, I have striven to remain faithful to my initial decision of presenting a series of reflections that will flow more easily and be less cluttered with quotations. Anyone who compares the various themes dealt with here, with what I wrote in the earlier study, will find that the first work contains a number of analyses and citations that reveal the foundation for what is stated in the present volume, although it, too, contains more than enough of them to clarify those foundations. But aside from this, the elements for consideration that have been introduced in this second work are enough to make of it a new contribution to theological reflection on the religious life.

ACKNOWLEDGMENT

We wish to thank Fr. Joseph Daries, C.M.F. for the decisive contribution he has made in the preparation of this book. Without him, the publication of this text in English would not have been possible.

I ‖ Introducing a Theme

Let us begin by delimiting the subject matter of these reflections. We are going to attempt to present an overall view of a phenomenon that appears in a number of Christian Churches, namely, the Catholic, Orthodox and Anglican communions and, to a lesser extent, certain Reformed Churches (Taizé, for example). During the last seven centuries, this phenomenon has been designated as the *religious life*. Earlier, however, especially during the eleventh and twelfth centuries, there was no single label to denote the full range of this phenomenon, and authors spoke, rather, of the *monastic life* and of the *canonical life*. Still earlier, we find it referred to exclusively as the *monastic life*, although it was known in two forms, the eremitical (lived in solitude) and the cenobitical (lived in community). The term "monastic" was first coined in order to designate solitaries ("monk" means "alone"), but it was soon (as early as the fourth century) extended in meaning to include those living apart from society, but in community (shared solitude). Certainly, neither St. Basil nor St. Macrina would have followed this terminology. Basil preferred the expression "life faithful to the Gospel." This expression, however, itself gives rise to not a few questions. By the time of Pius XII, there was a felt need for a new term that would embrace not only religious institutes and the somewhat similar societies of common life, but also the newly emerging secular institutes. The new term chosen—the *life of perfection*—was based on Thomas Aquinas' teaching concerning the "states of perfection." The new Code of Canon Law now speaks of "life consecrated by the profession of the evangelical counsels."[1] Once

3

again excluded from this terminology are societies of apostolic life, which the new code says "resemble" *(accedunt)* institutes of consecrated life.[2]

HISTORICAL VARIATIONS

The reason for these periodic changes lies precisely in the fact that the phenomenon we are dealing with belongs to the category of "life." We are talking about a type of Christian life—something that is far easier to intuit and describe than it is to define. This "life" or rather these kinds of life have emerged out of different kinds of societies, with different cultural horizons and concerns, and have hence tended to pursue largely divergent aims. New forms have continued to emerge throughout history, obliging us to invent new terms for them, pressing theologians to modify their points of view, and forcing canonists to change laws. This has happened above all in the Western (Roman or Anglican) Church, because in the Eastern Churches the religious life has been more faithful to monastic ideals.

Until the eleventh century, monasticism was, with a few fleeting exceptions (notably that of Augustine), the only form of religious life, and communities of priests tended to be assimilated to it. But the twelfth century saw the independent rise and flourishing of clerical communities dedicated to an itinerant life of preaching. Indeed, the twelfth century was a period of crisis for what came to be called the religious life, but for that very reason it was also a period of great creativity. This was the time of the appearance of centralized institutes founded for an external service, such as the Orders of Hospitalers, which cared for the sick and for pilgrims, and which eventually became military orders, in order to defend their charges. In France, toward the end of the twelfth century, the Order of the Most Holy Trinity was founded for the liberation of Christian prisoners from Muslim captivity. The thirteenth century developed these tendencies even further: institutes ordinarily had a central government and, after initially adopting an itinerant form of life, became more stabilized. While the Friars Minor continued with a traditional concept of the religious life, as a life (although with many structural changes), other groups were founded precisely for an active ministry (the Dominicans and Mercedarians). A third group (the Servites, Augustinians and Carmelites) would abandon the eremitical life in order to enter cities and unite their religious life with the ministry.

The phenomenon continued to manifest itself in a variety of forms. In the late Middle Ages, there were a number of local communities of the pious, whose members, both men and women, practiced what were then considered the essential requisites for the religious life, namely, celibacy, poverty and obedience, but on a rather spontaneous basis, without being bound by vows or the rigorous enclosure that had been imposed on religious women. Some of these communities would give rise to an institute: the Alexian Brothers.

The sixteenth century marked the beginning of another great period of creativity. First, there were the Clerks Regular who, along the lines of the canonical tradition, joined community life with priestly ministry, such as the latter had been developing for several centuries. St. Ignatius Loyola created a radically apostolic type of institute, the Company or Society of Jesus. While in the past other orders (such as the Dominicans, Trinitarians and Mercedarians) had been founded for the active ministry, now everything began to be derived from apostolic mission. ''To help souls'' became the byword and central criterion. Mary Ward wanted to do something similar for women, but the Church did not understand her. Around this time (perhaps in response to an exaggerated clericalization of the Church) came lay institutes, composed exclusively or mainly of non-ordained laypersons. Founded in the great majority of cases for some external service (originally for Christian education or the corporal works of mercy), most of them were women's groups. A short time later (the seventeenth century), the next group of institutes to enter the historical scene were made up of priests and brothers devoted more or less exclusively to itinerant preaching and the giving of retreats.

All of these institutes, for various reasons (in women's groups, so as to avoid incurring the law of enclosure), began to adopt a type of commitment called simple vows, which would not render acts contrary to them invalid, but only illicit. Since the Church has often been resistant to accepting new forms of the religious life, some institutes, such as the Daughters of Charity of St. Vincent de Paul, in order to protect their distinctive identity, decided to make only annual vows. Others, in contrast, such as the Oratory of St. Philip Neri, shied away from vows and spoke of charity as the only bond that held them together: societies of apostolic life had been born in the Church.

Everything seemed to be clear and definitively established, when along came the secular institutes. Although they were born around the time of the French Revolution, these new types of institution have multiplied throughout the present century. Secular institutes have created a new form of commitment. But what really distinguishes their tenor of life is the fact that, motivated by a desire to act from within civil society, their members do not profess a life in community.

Throughout this history of the evolution of what has until lately been called the religious life, one significant fact stands out. The new forms, although they tend to spread rapidly at the time of their appearance (because they respond better to the common needs and feeling of their times), and by that very fact bring about a lessening in the number of those who enter earlier groups, nevertheless do not lead to the death of these earlier groups. The kinds of solitaries who were predominant in the third century co-exist today with the members of secular institutes.

COMMON TRAITS

Periodically, in times of crisis and creativity, Christians have continued to ask what are the traits common to all these forms, since as one was suppressed, others were added. The question was debated in the eleventh and twelfth centuries, was revived in the nineteenth century, and has again come to the fore in our times under the rubric of "essential elements of the religious life."

Anyone who reflects on this very broad phenomenon is bound to ask what all these forms of life, created by religious experience, can possibly have in common. What can a person who lives in solitude, devoted to prayer and reflection, have in common with a doctor or a city mayor who belongs to a secular institute? What is there in common between a Trappistine, a Jesuit, a Daughter of Charity and a Brother of the Christian Schools? The reader will at once note that all of these last-mentioned people are committed to living a kind of life which can only be explained in terms of religious experience, that all of them make a commitment to celibacy (the early anchorites included this in their profession of solitude), and that all of them, historically, have laid great emphasis on a poverty inspired by evangelical ideals. More than this we cannot say, because, from this point on, the forms of life they have adopted differ considerably.

The primitive anchorites or solitaries lived in celibacy and poverty. The cenobites, from the fourth century onward, added community life and therefore obedience to the leader of the group, as a permanent trait of life. In apostolic institutes, the radical element, which creates all other elements, is the desire to respond to a need of the Church and of society through an active, public service. Moreover, this new element serves to differentiate the common traits received from earlier tradition, above all as regards the type of community life followed in the institute. Now secular institutes have again suppressed the profession of life in community, although they have kept the commitment of obedience in those matters that affect the life and works of the institution.

RELIGIOUS EXPERIENCE

In fact, all of these elements, whether it be the flight into solitude, the profession of celibacy, the decision to follow a life of poverty, the decision to enter a community and therefore to make a commitment of obedience, or the desire to live and die consecrated to a service on behalf of humanity and the Church, are all only expressions of something far deeper. These men and women have been touched by God, and this touch leads them to want to build a life which, in its very material shape, as a type of existence, has its explanation in the experience of God and tends to facilitate the further development of this experience.

Perhaps the best way to understand this is to put it in its overall natural and human context, which goes far beyond the frontiers of Christianity. The monachate came into existence in Buddhism and Jainism, some eight centuries before it did in the Christian world. And even before it appeared in Buddhism, Manichaeism was familiar with the distinction between the elect, who were "sealed" with the three seals of mouth, hands and breast (observing chastity, poverty and abstinence from flesh and wine), and the hearers, who supported the elect by works and alms. The monachate also appears, although only sporadically, in Israel, among certain groups of Essenes (Qumran), around the beginning of the Christian era. Some centuries later, in Islam, there arose a number of spiritual brotherhoods open to mystical experience (the Sufis), whose life and organization has certain points in common with the Christian monks of the East. If the priest appears in one form or another in most religions of the world, the monk and the nun appear only in special kinds of religious milieus. It has been said more than once that monasticism arises in salvation religions, that is, in those religions which perceive the human being as living in a situation which is contrary to his or her true vocation, and which offer themselves as the means of salvation from this threatening situation. Certainly, Buddhism and Christianity belong in this category. Judaism and Islam tend to issue into an eschatology, that is, into a doctrine concerning the end-time, for which they try to prepare their adepts. The idea of individual salvation is decisive in Buddhist monasticism, and throughout history it has often been a predominant reason why certain Christians have chosen the monastic life. But personal salvation does not seem to have played a decisive role in the vocations of St. Francis of Assisi or Teresa of Avila, or, as a general rule, in that of the Sufi mystics. What can often be seen is a desire for loving union with the divinity, by way of mystical experience. Moreover, the desire to help one's neighbor, rather than the thought of one's own future, has been the cause of the foundation of many religious institutes in the Catholic Church: the Dominicans, the Jesuits, the Sisters of the Good Shepherd and the Little Sisters of the Poor. For this reason, it is perhaps more accurate to say that the religious life arises in those religions that tend to facilitate in their followers an intense experience of the divine. And while there can be no doubt that many religions limit themselves to the performance of public religious rituals, there are others in which a personal, conscious relationship between human beings and the divine is absolutely basic. And there can be no doubt that Buddhism, Judaism, Christianity and Islam belong to this latter group.

The same underlying meaning comes through from even a cursory glance at the way individual persons make the decision to become religious. Aspirants (supposing them to be adults or young adults), usually after a period of inner resistance and tension, decide to consecrate their whole life to religion, even though this involves sacrificing some of their deepest human values, such as married love, motherhood or fatherhood. Ordinarily, too, aspirants (unless they opt for the eremitical life) sacrifice the free disposition of their person and, in some cases, the relative ease of a comfortable economic situation. They do so in response to an inner inclination (which Christians call a vocation or calling). Obviously, those who choose such a definitive state of life do so by getting in touch with that deep level of the psyche where serious decisions of this type are made. It will mean committing their *whole* person and their *whole* life. We are speaking, of course, of an initial decision, because a religious may later begin to hold back certain areas of his or her person or life. But for our purposes here (namely, to investigate the primary meaning of religious life), what counts is that basic intentionality whereby the person is fully oriented toward religious experience.

RELIGION AS A FORM OF LIFE

But that is not all there is to the matter, because in the salvation religions we have been speaking of, there are not a few persons whose lives are permeated with a deep religiosity (we say that some people are "very religious"), even though they are not "religious" in the technical sense in which we are using the word here. In Christianity (the milieu with which we are most familiar), there are also laypersons who decide to get married and adopt a civil profession, but do so on a deep faith-level, out of a desire to respond to a "call" from God. What is the difference, then, between laypersons of this sort and religious? Simply that those who are called "religious," in the technical sense of the word, have decided to adopt a way of life whose intrinsic, underlying explanation is religious experience. Marriage or any civil profession has its own self-contained motives, which do not of themselves require religious experience as their reason for being. Marriage is a deeply human reality which can be embraced by almost anyone, with or without faith. The same can be said of any civil profession, whether it be that of a doctor, a doorman, a teacher or a businessperson. If faith is involved in any of these options, it will be revealed by the way the person lives this matrimonial relationship or this particular occupation—but not by the very fact of choosing them for oneself. In contrast, the religious life is in itself, as the word implies, a type of existence that is expressly built around religious experience and which aims at manifesting that experience. A candidate becomes celibate "for the sake of the kingdom of God," that is, in order to live that kingdom fully and to manifest its presence in our midst. Without a deep religious decision, this type of existence would be bereft of all meaning.

The fact of being a religious is something visible. If you go to Thailand and ask the ordinary people who those men are, with the shaved heads and saffron tunics, begging for rice in the marketplace during the early hours of the morning, they will tell you that they are "Buddhist monks,'' individuals who live lives of total commitment to meditation and asceticism, in search of religious enlightenment. Among Christians—with their concept of a personal God who exists before us and of himself (from all eternity) and calls us out of love—the anchorites very early (around the beginning of the fourth century) began to be called the *manservants and maidservants of God,* and soon after this their life began to be defined as an existence committed to the service of God. This definition of the monachate as a life committed to the service of God entered into the mainstream of Christian tradition. Benedict popularized it when he described the monastery as "the school of service to the Lord."[3] St. Thomas took this way of understanding the religious life as the point of departure for his reflections on it. Echoes of his teaching and that of all the tradition before him reach as far as Vatican II.[4]

In the Bible—and, by that very fact, in Christianity—the relationship between the human being and the transpersonal God forms the central nucleus of all religious experience. Here God is perceived not only as reality and truth in itself, but as a reality who is personal, because by nature he *is* supreme consciousness and loving will. God is not simply a goal, but is also the source of the deepest messages, those messages that call us into being, that reveal the very meaning of existence, and call us to realize and actualize our existence in its fullness. Religion, and therefore the religious life, appear here as a response. However, the religious life is not an essential requisite for this relationship of faith, hope and love, because a lay Christian—that is to say, one who does not profess the religious life in the technical sense in which we are using the expression—can live with God in a relationship of faith that is more intense than that of many religious. We have already said that what distinguishes the religious life is the fact of its being a type of Christian existence which has its fundamental reason for being in religious experience—not in the spirit with which this relationship is lived. But it is quite clear that when the religious life ceases to be animated by this relationship with God, it loses its meaning.

We need to insist on this point. Religious do not dedicate their lives to affirming certain values (the "higher" value of heavenly goods or of eternity) or, on the negative side, to stress the transitory or "lower" character of other goods (earthly values). It is highly doubtful that the prospect of making such affirmations or negations would be enough to compel anyone to commit his or her whole life to them. Religious commit their persons and their lives to God. For this very reason, the religious life transcends the limits of any mere philosophy (although Christian writers of the fourth century, under the influence of pagan ascetical movements, often used the term ''philosophy'' to describe the underlying rationale of monasticism); for the essential thrust of the religious life is a relationship with God. Heaven and eternity are God, the God who reveals himself to us in history and, in a unique way, in the cross and glory of his Son and Servant, Jesus.

RELATIONSHIP WITH GOD

We have embarked upon a complex subject which is fraught with consequences, not only for a proper understanding of religiosity itself but, by implication, for those of us who have been called to the religious life: a type of existence that is not only created by this relationship with God, but aimed at manifesting it publicly.

Throughout history there have been and still are various ways of understanding this relationship with God, or, in a broader sense, with the divine. One very common way is that which sees this relationship in a sacralizing sense. In most of the religious systems that favor this approach, the divinity does not create or found the universe. Rather, various gods and goddesses form part of the world (Uranus, the sky and Gaea, the earth, for example), and possess only some part of it. Human beings enter into relationship with them, basically, by separating something in their environment for the use of honor of these divinities: a temple, an animal (which is either sacrificed or simply considered sacred), a day, a particular rite, or a person (who is likewise either sacrificed or simply considered sacred, set apart). In such systems, there is a neat distinction between the sacred (which belongs to the divinity) and the profane (that which does not belong to the divinity). It is interesting to note that in a number of languages, what is related to the divinity is indicated by terms whose roots signify separating or setting apart (*sacer* in Latin, *qdsh* in Hebrew, and possibly *hagios* in Greek). This way of understanding the relationship with the divine is reflected in the more archaic strata of the religious history of Israel, and it had to be purified considerably by the prophets. Obviously, this way of understanding our relationship with God could not, logically, be maintained, once it had been clearly established that God is the Creator of all things, that all things come from

God and that all things belong to God. Yet despite this, even in Christianity we often run the risk of falling under the influence of this archaic way of understanding the relationship with God, whenever we speak of the priesthood or of worship, especially when we set out from a base that is supposedly common to "all" religions.

Another way of understanding the relationship with God or the divine derives from considering God purely as absolute transcendence, so that God is seen as irreconcilable with the world and with history. Here, there are two possibilities. One can optimistically opt for some kind of secularized humanism: human beings fulfill their mission simply by being true to the values that reason discovers and by faithfully conforming their behavior to these values. Only in this way can a good man or woman live in harmony with that transcendent reality, the unknown God. In contrast, one can opt for a pessimistic view of the reality in which we find ourselves immersed. Here, the relationship with God or the transcendent Being can only be dealt with by way of renunciation and evasion. This attitude, in turn, may be based on two diverse views of reality.

One of these world-views is ontological dualism, which regards the reality that surrounds us as being in opposition to the Absolute: everything that surrounds us and affects us from without is pure illusion (Buddhism), a mere shadow of the ideal world (Platonism), an inferior and contemptible reality which prevents us from being our true selves (gnostic dualism), or a product of the evil principle (Manichaeism). In all systems of this sort, human beings do not belong to the world and are not corporeal beings, although they are imprisoned in the body. Although these religious systems obviously do not jibe with Christianity, they have occasionally affected the way in which religious life is understood. This tends to happen whenever renunciation occupies a central place in spirituality.

The other vision of reality consists of a dynamic and successive dualism which contrasts the human present, viewed as an oppressive situation, with the liberating future that will be created by the power or grace of God: eschatological dualism. Iranian religion seems to have been the cradle of this way of viewing the present and the future. Independently of its own earlier eschatological tradition, Israel developed a strong current of eschatological speculation and spirituality in the intertestamental period. The conviction that God was going to liberate Israel and establish his kingdom was at fever pitch among Jews at that time. We should not forget that Jesus himself appeared precisely as an eschatological prophet, the herald of the reign of God. There was, both in him and in his message, a tension between the human present and the divine future, which we will later have to analyze.

St. Thomas Aquinas, who fully re-established human being in the world by affirming that the soul is not merely the driver of a body conceived after the manner of a cart, but is the truly constitutive principle of the human body as human, reminds us that, in consequence of this, all of our ideas about God (we would add, all of our religious symbols) proceed from our experience of things in the world and of the history of salvation.[5] This points toward a fundamental fact: it is impossible to relate oneself to God through a process of annulling or negating the world. Human beings, as human, are part of the world and their experience always proceeds from the reality of which they form a part. Transcending ourselves in order to reach the transcendent God can only mean penetrating the reality in which we live to its very depths, and leading this same reality back to those depths.

Perhaps it was unnecessary for us to place ourselves on this level of philosophical reflection. The Bible would have been enough: God, the transcendent Creator, has revealed himself to us in our own history, that is to say, in the world and in a particular way in human being. This revelation culminates and takes on a unique character in Christ Jesus. Our relationship with God cannot do without the history of humankind. It has to pass through it. Every attempt to the contrary tends to negate, either explicitly or implicitly, biblical revelation and in a special way the revelation of God in Jesus.

Even on the philosophical level it is a highly questionable assertion, to say the least, that human beings are capable of their own unaided efforts to reach God. But even if this were possible, it would still be highly questionable, to say the least, to imagine that God could be reached simply by renouncing everything and emptying oneself. But aside from all this, the Bible tells us two things: first, that God reveals himself to us in our own history, and, second, that we are all under the grace of God, who calls and draws us. The Christian contemplation of God, and, by that very fact, our relationship with God, takes its starting point in history, in a unique way, in a re-encounter with Jesus, who died and is risen.

THE HORIZONS CHANGE

The religious life has existed in the Church for many centuries. In its anchoritic or primitive eremitical form, it has existed since the end of the third century. We know that even before this there were Christian ascetics. And we believe that the origins of the religious life go back to Paul, who freely chose celibacy for apostolic reasons, and even to those itinerant prophets who preached the return of the Son of Man, relinquishing their families and occupation in order to do so.

Throughout the long course of time, what we today call the religious life has moved along a diversity of cultural and theological horizons, and has naturally been affected by them. Bear with us as we cast a rapid historical glance over these horizons (with all the limitations that rapidity entails), in order to take stock of some of these variations.

From the end of the third century and throughout the fourth, solitude was the very basis of monasticism, the factor that allowed it to exist as such. The anchorites spoke of choosing between God and human beings, and they fled from society. They devoted themselves to prayer and work, and practiced harsh forms of asceticism. A certain number of them—laypersons who, as their biographers tell us, never saw a human face for years and years—did not partake in the Eucharist throughout this whole period. The Psalms and the Christian Scriptures were their spiritual sustenance. But many of them soon discovered the religious value of interpersonal relationships and began to consult with one another. Some groups set up colonies where it was easier to get together periodically in order to listen to an exhortation, to pray and to celebrate the Eucharist. Pachomius, moved by the desire to help his brothers, created real towns of brothers and discovered the spirituality of communion. He was followed in this by his sister Mary. Basil, converted to a fervent life by his sister Macrina, recalled that the important thing was being Christian, and asked himself just what evangelical meaning this whole phenomenon of the monachate might have. His response was to create small fraternities. But the fact that he so intensely disliked speaking of "monks," as opposed to "Christians," makes it very difficult for us to understand the nature of the relationship between those who committed themselves to celibacy and community, and the rest of the faithful in his scheme of things. In North Africa, Augustine placed fraternal communion in the very center of a life committed to the service of God. Here, the important thing was to form one single heart oriented toward God. Although his work was strongly inspired in the New Testament, one can discover in it at least some marginal influences from Neoplatonic and Neopythagorean groups. But after so many years spent as a priest and later as a bishop, Augustine did not fall into the temptation of considering his brotherhood as making up the perfect Church. He simply aimed at reviving, in the service of others, something of the "paradise lost" that presumably existed in the Church immediately after Pentecost. From yet another standpoint, it should be noted here that, both in Basil and in Augustine, asceticism ceases to be the central issue in monasticism.

The basis for the theoretical explanation of what we now call the religious life was given by the early authors of Neoplatonically inspired treatises on virginity. The gist of what these authors had to say was that the original vocation of humanity, that of our "paradise lost," was virginity. Monks and nuns were the only ones capable of following the unique Christian calling (to virginity). The monastic life was, then, the life of the perfect, of the strong. Simultaneously, either out of a defensive reaction or out of pessimism, stress was laid on the world as a situation of danger and of sin. This is clearly seen in the *Rule of the Master*, toward the beginning of the sixth century. St. Benedict corrected this and attempted to create an ideal situation in which seekers could learn to serve God fittingly.

These philosophical horizons within which monasticism had been moving began to undergo ever deeper changes in the twelfth century, with the ongoing rediscovery of nature that took place throughout that period. Relationships between religious and laypersons were now easier, and one result of this new easiness was the founding of Third Orders. But the distinction of classes was to some extent still maintained because of the scholastic formulation of the religious state as a state in search of perfection, and therefore as a state superior to that of the laity. The theology of religious life accentuated individualism (the quest for personal perfection), which had come from primitive anchorism. The Augustinian balance between person and community had found few imitators. Then came the founding of the first institutes established specifically for an external ministry. But, on the one hand, the weight of the monastic tradition was too great and, on the other, there was the long-standing Hellenistic interpretation of the human being as one called primarily to the contemplation of immutable being and truth.

Hence, it was not until the time of Ignatius Loyola that the ideal of "helping souls" could be set in the very center of the religious life. Now the world was also America and Asia, and religious institutes began to discover a missionary vocation. Vincent de Paul gave a mystical interpretation to action, with his recommendation "to be passive in action." The feminism of the French *siècle d' or* made it possible for women to assume public ministries (although they were not called that at the time). It seemed that the religious life was standing at the brink of a new era.

But the movement ground to a halt. Trent vigorously reimposed on all women religious the law of enclosure that had been prescribed by Boniface VIII (1294–1303) and Benedict XII (1334–1342). The influence which monasticism and conventual life had exerted on apostolic institutes, joining company with a spirituality marked by a Jansenist distrust in human values (freedom, friendship), reinstated sacrifice and austerity as the very hub of the religious life. A negative, puritanical view of sexuality left its mark on the way of understanding celibacy.

New and profound changes in cultural horizons (freedom, personalism, solidarity, the rediscovery of earthly values, new psychological theories, etc.) had been internally eroding the traditional image of the religious life. Finally, it all came out into the public when Vatican II called for the spiritual renewal and adaptation of the religious life to modern circumstances. We began to look at God's world in a more positive way, we laid greater stress on interpersonal relationships and on interacting with lay Christians, and obedience began to be purified of many of its former ideological incrustations.

A RETURN TO JESUS, THE NORM AND CRITERION

We have already seen how the monachate overflows, both in time and space, the boundaries of Christianity. It is fitting that in our days, when the planet is tending toward unification, Buddhist and Christian monks should be dialoguing on their respective religious experiences. But what is most certain is that monasticism, like every other form of Christian religious life, cannot come to an understanding of itself without returning to face up to the experience and the message that gave rise to Christianity.

Vatican II has defined the renewal of the religious life as a "return [that is, of the religious life as such, and not just of individuals] to the sources of all Christian life,'' namely, ''to the following of Christ as set forth in the Gospels.'' Christ, his life, his ministry and his message constitute the supreme norm and ultimate criterion of authenticity. Although the Council document refers to the practice of the religious life, it is clear that its recommendation can and should be applied to the theology of this type of Christian life. A renewal of the theology of the religious life, returning to the experience of Jesus as its determinant criterion, is indispensable for this renewal of religious life itself. This is even more necessary at present, for two basic reasons.

In the first place—partly because we are in a period of creative crisis (and therefore distanced from our immediate past) and partly because our historical sensitivity is sharper today—we have taken stock of the periodic oscillations that the religious life has undergone under the influence of factors that are not precisely Christian. This is quite normal. Can anyone be unaware that the religious life is itself an historical reality? But this obliges us to ask ourselves, as Basil of Caesarea did, ''What evangelical meaning is there to all of this?''

In the second place, we find ourselves today somewhat without moorings. The theory of our life as a ''state of perfection to be acquired'' was set aside by the Council, yet the Council did not give us (it was not a task for the Council, anyway) a systematic vision of the religious life. This new situation obliges us to rethink our attitude toward the world, our relationships with the great lay Church, and so on. And all of this obliges us to return to the original source of our inspiration. That is what we are going to attempt to do, starting with the following chapter.

Notes

1. CIC, can. 373.
2. CIC, can. 731.
3. RB, Prol. 46.
4. LG, 44; PC, 5, 9, 12.
5. 1 q 8 a 7 ad 1.

Bibliography

L. Boff, *God's Witnesses in the Heart of the World* (Chicago: Claret Center for Resources in Spirituality, 1981) pp. 3–80. On religious experience.

L. Cada *et al.*, *Shaping the Coming Age of Religious Life* (New York: Seabury, 1979) pp. 11–50. On the various forms of religious life.

B. Hume, *Searching for God* (New York: Paulist, 1978). The monastic vision.

G.A. Lane, *Christian Spirituality. An Historical Sketch* (Chicago: Loyola University Press, 1984) pp. 45–50, 55–60. The apostolic horizons.

D.E. Fleming, ed., *Religious Life at the Crossroads* (New York: Paulist, 1985). The present situation in the United States.

II | Jesus, In Whom It All Began

In comparing the historical phenomenon of the Christian religious life with the original experience that gave rise to Christianity (Jesus, his person, his life, his ministry, his message), two possible methods are available. One is the "descending" method: from the Gospel to history. In this method, one goes to the New Testament to find there some words or deeds that apparently justify the root-origins of the religious life or some of its fundamental traits. This is the method that has been in general use until recent decades. But both history and New Testament criticism have increasingly disclosed the deficiencies of this method. It is frequently based on a naive reading of Scripture and sometimes on tendentious interpretations. In the past, for example, a number of legislators of the religious life pounced on the *logion* "He who hears you, hears me" (Lk 10:16), in order to provide a scriptural basis for the authority of superiors. One writer (the author of the *Rule of the Master*) went so far as to see in this text the institution of a hierarchy of abbots, alongside that of bishops! Ordinarily, too, there was a rather "literal" reading (based on a number of Hellenistic suppositions) of texts dealing with the renunciation of this world's goods.

In fact, however, the basic fallacy of this descending method (from the Gospels to history) did not consist so much in its projection of later thought-patterns on scriptural texts, as it did in its attempt to attribute to Jesus the express will of establishing a particular and permanent state of life among those who received his message. The same trend can be seen even recently in those ecclesiologies that have rather stubbornly insisted

19

on attributing to the historical Jesus the express project of establishing a Church. But the relationship between the Church and various kinds of Christian life, on the one hand, and Jesus, on the other, is of another sort. It was with the death and resurrection of Jesus (as the Fathers themselves had already said) that the prophetic group of disciples was converted into a Church.

This leaves us with the other, "ascending" method: from history to the Gospel. Since the religious life is a phenomenon that has appeared and developed in history, we must go back to that life to see if and in what manner the remembrance of Jesus (the *memoria Jesu*) figured in the religious experience of those who started this kind of life with its various forms and institutions. This will allow us to assess the degree to which the life of Jesus, consecrated to the proclamation of the reign of God, was or was not the creative source that inspired them, and whether the inspired text had any real influence on them. Only then, in a second phase of investigation, should these texts be scrutinized in themselves, to see whether there is a valid connection between them and what has been created in history.

THE FACTS

In the case we are considering, history is both unequivocal and persistent. Throughout it, one fact is repeated over and over again. It appears as early as the *Life of Antony,* the great anchorite, written by Athanasius shortly after the death of his hero (352 A.D.). This is quite significant, because the *Vita Antonii* is in fact the first treatise on monastic spirituality and the first rule of life written for anchorites. Athanasius tells us how Antony "discovered" this life which, according to him, was a new one among Christians. As he was on his way to church one day, the young Antony began thinking of how the apostles had left all to follow Jesus, and how the Jerusalem faithful had sold all their goods and put the money they gained at the disposal of the apostles. As he was still turning these matters over in his mind, he entered the church during the reading of the Gospel, at that passage where the Lord told the rich young man: "If you would be perfect, go, sell what you possess and give to the poor, and you will have treasure in heaven; and come, follow me" (Mt 19:21 and par.). As if these words had been addressed to him personally, Antony, upon leaving church, sold his goods and began leading an ascetical life that soon culminated in his going into solitude.

We are dealing here, obviously, with the Hellenistic literary genre of the exemplary biography. Thus it is not certain that Antony had these very facts and sayings in his memory at the particular moment when he discovered his vocation. What is certain, however, is that these were the facts and texts in which the early monks felt the call to follow this distinctive way of life. In this connection, Athanasius reminds his readers of the texts of the call of the disciples, of the summaries in Acts dealing with renouncing goods for the sake of the poor and, in a central way, of the words addressed to the rich man in Mt 19:21, which are also a text on the call to follow Jesus. Jerome did much the same in his account of the calling of the monk Hilarion. He, too, cites Mt 19:21 and the summaries from Acts, adding the text of Lk 14:33 ("None of you can be my disciple if he does not renounce all his possessions"). The author of the lives of Hypatios and Cyriacus tells us that the former discovered his vocation under the influence of Mt 19:21, while the latter was moved by Lk 9:23 ("If any man would come after me, let him deny himself and take up his cross daily and follow me"). In the sayings of the Desert Fathers, Abbot Pambo cites both Mt 19:21 and Lk 9:23 in a similar context. Later (toward the beginning of the sixth century), the *Rule of the Master* cites Mt 19:21 a number of times, either alone or with Lk 14:33, precisely in speaking of the entrance of aspirants into the monastic life.

Centuries later, during another period of great creativity, the Franciscan Rule of 1221 begins precisely by citing Mt 19:21, along with other texts of Christian radicalism (Mt 16:24; Lk 14:16; Mt 19:29). The first question in the Examen concerning the dispositions of aspirants to the Society of Jesus ("Whether he is determined to leave the world and follow the counsels of Christ our Lord")[1] alludes above all to Mt 19:21, as can be seen from parallel passages in Jesuit documents.[2] The following of Christ is the fundamental idea in the "ideal description of a Claretian," written by their founder.

In other instances, remembrance of these same Gospel texts abounds in passages dealing with particular aspects of the religious life, such as the initial renunciation of goods. This can be seen in the *Rule of the Master*,[3] in the *Bullata* of St. Francis,[4] in the Rule of St. Clare,[5] in the Constitutions of the Society of Jesus,[6] and in the primitive Rules and Constitutions of the Sisters of the Presentation.

One conclusion can clearly be drawn from this examination of fundamental documents of the religious life. The Gospel texts on the calling of the first disciples of Jesus and on the conditions required for following him have played a constant and decisive role in the creation of the religious life, from the primitive monachate to the apostolic institutes. This fact appears in historical association with another: the religious life has traditionally been viewed as a privileged expression (in what sense, we will have to determine later) of the vocation to follow the Lord. Pachomius had already (fourth century Egypt) laid down as a golden rule for his brothers: "Follow the Lord in all things."[7] Basil of Caesarea wrote, a short time later, that what counts is to respond in truth to the call of Christ who invites us to follow him bearing the cross.[8] Jerome invites Rusticus to follow in nakedness the naked Christ.[9] For this very reason, the monachate soon came to be called the apostolic life, that is, a life in imitation of that led by the disciples of Jesus. Basil, referring basically to the same fact, chose rather to call it the faithful observance of the Gospel.

In our own day, Vatican II summed up this long tradition in its description of the religious life as a type of existence which more closely imitates and reproduces the way that the Lord followed and proposed to his disciples.[10] In the decree *Perfectae Caritatis,* the Council refers to those men and women who, since the beginning of the Church, have decided to follow Christ with greater liberty[11] and speaks of the following of Christ as the primary end of the religious life,[12] of the special profession of religious,[13] of their vocation,[14] and of the supreme norm of the religious life.[15]

Each of the two facts we have just described (the influence of Gospel texts on the *sequela Christi,* and the interpretation of the religious life as a special way of fulfilling the call to Christian discipleship) gives rise to problems that are both serious and difficult to solve. The first obliges us to investigate, by way of a critical reading of the Gospel texts, whether the reading done by so many men and women disciples of Jesus, when they began the various forms of religious life, has a valid relation to the intrinsic thrust of those texts. The second obliges us to ask ourselves about the relationship between the religious life and other forms of Christian life, because it is also a fact that Vatican II, shortly before dealing with religious, calls all Christians "followers of Christ"[16] and earlier refers to them as "disciples of Christ."[17] What relation is there, then, between that distinctive mode of following which is the religious life, and the common vocation of all Christians?

TEXTS ON THE FOLLOWING

In the Gospels we find several series of passages dealing with the vocation of the disciples of Jesus (in the twofold sense of being called and of a distinctive way of life). In all these passages the concept of "following" (*akolouthein* = to follow) is central. Moreover, the word for "disciples" (*mathetai* = learners) refers to those who follow Jesus.

(A) First series. Made up of sayings attributed to the Lord, relating to the condition of disciples, that is, to the fundamental traits that should characterize their existence.

1. Preeminent among these is a saying to which the first churches must have attached great importance, since it is found both in the Q Source (used by Matthew and Luke) and in the tradition collected by Mark and repeated by the other two Synoptics. In the Q version in Luke we read: "Whoever does not bear his own cross and come after me cannot be my disciple" (Lk 14:27 = Mt 10:38. Cf. Mk 8:36 and par.).

Coupled with this Q saying, there is another on family ties vis-à-vis the following of Jesus. In its original form it may have read: "Whoever does not hate his father and mother, cannot be my disciple. Whoever does not hate his son and his daughter cannot be my disciple" (Lk 14:26 = Mt 10:37).

2. Besides this, there are a few texts from Q (common to Matthew and Luke) on an uprooted kind of life and on rupturing family ties. Matthew has two of these sayings: "Foxes have holes, and birds of the air have nests; but the Son of man has nowhere to lay his head. . . . Follow me, and leave the dead to bury their own dead" (Mt 8:18–22). Luke repeats the first saying, modifies the second ("Leave the dead to bury their own dead; but as for you, go and proclaim the kingdom of God"), and adds a third: "No one who puts his hand to the plow and looks back is fit for the kingdom of God" (Lk 9:57–62).

(B) Second series. Made up of texts narrating the call issued to different disciples.

1. In the Synoptics we have Jesus' call of the first four disciples (Mk 1:16–20 = Mt 4:18–22; cf. Lk 5:1–11), and that of Levi-Matthew (Mk 2:13–17 and par.). Then, also in the Synoptics, we have the call of the rich young man who decided not to follow Jesus (Mk 10:21 and par.), followed, in reaction, by Peter's description of the attitude of the disciples (Mk 10:28 and par.).

2. In the Fourth Gospel we find an account of the disciples of the Baptizer who walk behind Jesus (Jn 1:37–40), followed by the call of Philip (Jn 1:43). Both of these Johannine passages add the distinctive nuance of the disciples' calling others in turn (Andrew inviting Cephas in Jn 1:41, and Philip inviting Nathanael in Jn 1:45–46).

(C) Third series. In the Johannine writings we find a number of texts dealing directly with the relationship between Jesus and believers.

1. In the Fourth Gospel we have the statement of Jesus, the Light: "He who follows me will not walk in darkness" (Jn 8:12), and of Jesus, the Good Shepherd: "the sheep follow him, for they know his voice. . . . My sheep hear my voice, and I know them, and they follow me" (Jn 10:4, 27).

2. Then, in the Apocalypse of John there is the passage about the undefiled "who follow the Lamb wherever he goes" (Rev 14:4).

We would like to call attention to two facts, the first of which is clear even to those not initiated in the meanderings of New Testament exegesis. The evangelists, and after them the churches for which they wrote, attribute great importance to "following Christ," that is, to being his disciple. In effect, we are here dealing with one of the key concepts of New Testament spirituality. The second fact is revealed to us by New Testament criticism: there is no reason not to attribute to Jesus himself the sayings on the conditions necessary for following him. Even the most demanding critics (Bultmann, for example) attribute Lk 9:62 ("No one who puts his hand to the plow . . .") to Jesus, and see no reason whatever for attributing Lk 9:58 ("Foxes have holes . . .") to the Church. Although other critics dissent, Lk 14:27 has for Bultmann a clearly pre-resurrection ring to it. Joachim Jeremias discovers the personal style of Jesus in some of these sayings. We are, then, in the presence of a cluster of traditions that bring us very close to the historical Jesus.

THE DISCIPLES OF JESUS

The Gospels tell us that Jesus had a strong impact on the popular masses of Israel. They frequently refer to the multitudes that *followed* him. At other times they relate how an individual person accepts his message and in this sense becomes one of his followers. But within the multitude, the Gospels single out the group of men and women who *followed* him (cf. Lk 8:1–3). The reference is to individuals whom he had called (the Synoptic vocation accounts, together with Jn 21:19, 22, insist on this) or at least accepted (Jn 1:35–42). It is not so easy, however, to reconstruct the characteristics of this group of close followers who accompanied Jesus throughout his ministry up to the passion. It seems to have been a relatively numerous group (cf. Lk 8:1–3 and Acts 1:22–24). That Jesus should have traveled about accompanied by a group of disciples fits very well with his historical milieu. The rabbis, too, had their disciples. So did John the Baptizer. But there was a deep difference between the disciples of Jesus and those of the famous rabbis. The latter came simply to learn, with a view to later becoming masters themselves, and of succeeding the one who had initiated them into the religious reading and interpretation of the law. Now Jesus, too, acted as a teacher, giving his own special interpretation of the torah; but he did so acting as the eschatological prophet, the servant anointed by the Spirit in order to proclaim the in-breaking of the kingdom of God. Hence, his disciples were more like those of the Baptizer. The latter accepted the message of John and associated themselves with him in imminent expectation of the day of the Lord. After his death they became followers of the religious movement that the Baptist had promoted during his lifetime.

Why did Jesus wish to have a group of disciples accompanying him? We cannot rule out his not wanting to be alone in facing the great coming which he hoped for and proclaimed (something similar must have moved the Baptist). There was a group of people who felt close to Jesus, and to whom he was able to communicate his hopes and ideas on the way to prepare for the kingdom of God. But we cannot attribute to him the project of creating with them a community separate from Israel. His message was addressed to all Israel, beginning with those who seemed to be farthest from the grace of God. The Gospels insist on the fact that he called them to collaborate with him in the proclamation of the kingdom of God and in the healings in which grace was beginning to reveal its presence. Mark speaks of the call of the first four disciples (Mk 1:16–20) immediately after presenting a summary of the prophetic message of Jesus: "The time is fulfilled, and the kingdom of God is at hand; repent, and believe in the Gospel" (Mk 1:15). In fact, the Synoptics tell us of a mission of the twelve in which the latter repeat the same message as Jesus and heal many sick (Mk 6:6b–13 and par.). Luke adds a second mission carried out by seventy-two disciples (Lk 10:1–12). Speaking of the twelve, Mark tells us that Jesus chose them to be his companions and that they were sent out by him to preach, with the power to expel demons (Mk 3:14).

Jesus did not, then, call his disciples to offer him worship. He never put himself at the center of his action or his message. He was the servant called to proclaim the grace that was beginning to be manifested, and his whole life, ministry and message were centered on this one thing: the reign of God. The disciples were called in order to face the advent of this saving event alongside Jesus, and, with him, to proclaim it. Following Jesus, then, meant standing alongside him before the merciful love of his heavenly Father. But we would be missing something very important if we did not grasp the importance which their relationship with Jesus came to assume in the experience of the disciples. Jesus gathered them together and continued communicating to them his most vivid faith, his experience of his Abba, as goodness without limit, as love which pardons and which, like all love, is extremely demanding. A type of religious experience developed between them and the Master. Moreover, Jesus himself came to constitute an essential part of the message he was preaching, because the kingdom was dawning in his person, in his preaching and in the cures he worked. Recent criticism has recognized an implicit, though clear, Christology in the message of Jesus or, if you like, a Christology in action. It is here that the future Church would have its roots, although all of this would take on a new meaning in the light of the resurrection.

It is to this group that some of the sayings we referred to above, concerning the following of Jesus, certainly refer in their original sense. This is true, for example, of the statement about not having a place to lay his head, about leaving the dead to bury their dead and, in all probability, the one about putting one's hand to the plow and looking back, although this saying obviously had a broader scope and could refer to all who accepted the message of conversion and faith that Jesus preached.

The same can be said of the serious warning contained in the saying on carrying the cross if one wanted to be a disciple. The cross, the chastisement of last resort reserved by the Romans for slaves and rebels, and used with some frequency in Israel at that time (Jesus himself would die by crucifixion), was not yet the redeeming cross, but rather was still simply a cruel and humiliating form of punishment.

THE DISCIPLES AS PARADIGM

The Gospels do not simply give us a few facts or sayings referring to the group of men and women who accompanied Jesus during his ministry. In the tradition from which the Gospels arose, the disciples had been transformed into the exemplary personification of those who believed in Christ after Easter. For Matthew, Mark and Luke, the historical group of disciples personified the Church which later came into being. John commonly skips over this mediating role (although traces of it can be found in him), in order to convert his Gospel into a series of messages addressed by the Word of God in his glory to the community of believers. He uses the verb *follow* to describe directly, sometimes in a metaphorical way, the relationship of the believer to the glorified Christ: the sheep follow their Shepherd. In Revelation, the virgins (those who have kept themselves undefiled by idolatry) follow the Lamb wherever he goes.

The fact that the Synoptics took the group that accompanied Jesus as a symbol of the whole Church, born of the cross and the resurrection, is something that must be kept carefully in mind for an understanding of the meaning that these sayings and facts take on when they are set forth in the first three Gospels. No longer was it a matter of describing the uprooted type of life led by the first disciples, since most believers now lived in their homes with their families. Nor was it a matter of reproducing the difficulties felt by Peter and the rest at having to leave their families to embark on their great adventure. The word of God is given to us in the Bible, with the sense that these sayings and deeds have in the sacred books. Theological reflection should start here, although the understanding of the original, pre-biblical meaning of these deeds and sayings might inspire us to see certain relationships between what obtains today (the religious life) and what Jesus was attempting to do during his ministry (calling disciples). But we must never forget that what really moved founders and foundresses, and what moves us today, is the memory of Jesus, of his actions (calling) and of the conditions he requires for discipleship, as all of these are found in the Gospels.

THE ACCOUNTS OF THE CALLING

The teaching of the Gospels on the value of the following of Christ in his expectation and proclamation of the reign of God, as well as on the conditions which this attitude of hope and service imposes on those called, is not found only in the sayings of Jesus. The primitive tradition of the Church has also embodied this in the various accounts on the call of some of the disciples. These accounts, although they refer to events that took place, are also charged with teaching and have hence been idealized. In very brief form, they all tell us basically the same thing: some men are immersed in their everyday affairs (fishing, collecting taxes, relating to one another in their families), when an apparently unknown man passes through their lives, addresses them with a few short words (*come after me* in Aramaic, *follow me* in Greek) and they leave everything—family and occupation—and go off with him. As an event in a chronicle, it would not make any sense. But it is not just any "unknown man" who passes through the account: for early tradition and for the evangelists who wrote it down and gave it shape, this man is the Christ, now risen and exalted, who passes through the lives of men and women calling them to faith, the only one who could have the authority to move us to abandon our past and our present. History has been used and idealized, in order to give us a message.

After underlining that the initiative comes from the Lord, and after demonstrating the unique authority with which he can and does intervene in our lives (a single word of his changes those lives), the account describes the response of those who are called: immediately (Mk 1:18) they leave their nets, or leave their father Zebedee in the boat with the hired hands, and follow him. The culminating point in these accounts is the word of Christ: "Follow me." The disciples' response is equally terse: "They followed him." The center of it all is relationship with Christ, understood, of course, in a post-resurrection sense, when these accounts were shaped as an expression of faith in the Son of God.

But note, too, that the response of the disciples itself contains an element of abandonment: they left their nets, they left their father (Mk 1:18, 20); Levi "rose," that is, he left his place behind the tax collector's counter (Mk 2:14). In the account of the rich man who did not accept the call, this negative aspect of leaving the situation in which one lives has been incorporated—the only case in which this is done—in the words with which Jesus calls him: "Go, sell what you have, and give to the poor . . . and come, follow me" (Mk 10:21). Peter's reaction expresses the matter radically: "We have left everything and followed you" (Mk 10:28). Here, it is not a question of leaving just their boats or even their father Zebedee or the tax collector's counter, but *everything*. The following of Christ demands a radical break. Luke took over this concept in order to stress the totality of the renunciation involved. Restructuring the material of the passage, he wrote that Peter, James and John, when they had brought their boats to land, "left everything and followed him" (Lk 5:11). Levi, too, "left everything, and rose and followed him" (Lk 5:28). As a conclusion to the sayings of Jesus on the demands of following him, Luke himself seems to have coined this radical statement: "So therefore, whoever of you does not renounce all that he has cannot be my disciple" (Lk 14:33).

These accounts significantly coincide with the sayings attributed to Jesus. In the latter, too, following Jesus entails the breaking of family ties. Recall, in this connection, the sayings about letting the dead bury their dead, and on having to prefer Jesus to father, mother, son and daughter, in order to be able to be a disciple (Lk 14:26; Mt 10:37). Here the disciples leave their family (in Aramaic, the family is the father's house, into which his wife is incorporated) and their work (the boat and the counter are not goods, but rather a means of gaining one's livelihood and of acting socially). From now on, they will have a higher profession: to be fishers of men (Lk 5:10). Jesus himself states that from that time on, his own family will be made up of "whoever does the will of God," that is, all who are converted and believe in the good news of the kingdom (Mk 3:35).

THE MEANING OF RENUNCIATION

It is clear enough, in these sayings and accounts, what "following Christ" means. Historically, it meant accepting his prophetic mission, and entering into a communion of faith and ministry with him. Starting with the Easter experiences that gave origin to the Church, the kingdom began to be identified with Christ the Lord, with his death and resurrection, and finally with his return as the Son of Man. Relationship with him became Christian faith. The disciples had been aware of encountering the grace of God when Jesus crossed their path. Afterward, they would understand more clearly that, in Jesus, God was making his definitive offer of salvation. To follow Jesus, then, would henceforward mean (and this is the sense in which the word is used in the Gospels) to believe in him, in his person as Son of God, and to accept his message of redeeming grace.

It is harder to understand what is meant by these sayings and narratives when they speak of leaving, denying, renouncing or abandoning things or persons for the sake of the kingdom. It should be noted that the sayings of Jesus on following him are couched in terms of a radical renunciation. They affect the two most incisive elements in the development of human life: disciples are to leave not only their own family, but also the work in which they would ordinarily build their lives and make their contribution to society. More than this, they must be prepared to renounce their own life, paradoxically saving it by losing it for Christ (Mt 10:39), and must take up their cross (Mt 10:38b). Peter (Mk 10:28 and par.) can say unhesitatingly that the disciples have abandoned everything (What more could they have to lose?) and Luke makes this point systematically in Luke-Acts. The account of the call issued to the rich young man includes a demand that he sell his possessions and give to the poor in order to become a disciple (Mk 10:21), and Luke, in his special material on the conditions for discipleship, concludes: "So, therefore, whoever of you does not renounce all that he has cannot be my disciple" (Lk 14:33).

If we return to the original sense of these passages, we will see that Jesus, in the general sayings attributed to him, did not ask everyone to give up riches, although his statements on the danger of riches and on the practical impossibility for the rich to enter the kingdom of God at least implicitly require a certain attitude of renunciation. But it is likewise certain that the disciples did not sell all their goods, since the women who followed Jesus supported him out of their goods (cf. Mk 15:41 = Mt 27:55), and the men returned to their boats (cf. Jn 21:2–3). Nor did Christ demand that they in fact break all ties with their families. He did not ask Peter to separate from his wife, and even went to his house with him (Mk 1:29 and par.). It is possible that the house of Peter and Andrew in Capernaum was the place where Jesus rested during his ministry around Lake Gennesaret. Still less did Jesus ask that they unthinkingly put themselves in danger of losing their lives, as other leaders seem to have done in their zeal to arouse the poor against the Romans.

There can be no doubt, however, that the disciples of Jesus, in order to be associated with him and cooperate with him in his prophetic ministry, had to make not a few sacrifices in their family life and had to leave their trade as fishers or tax collectors. The thing that primarily defined their existence was being disciples and co-workers of Jesus. Their hope in the imminent coming of the kingdom doubtless made their burdens lighter, but the accounts of the calling of the disciples are not concerned with making this point. Rather, these accounts have a universal scope, since they treat the disciples as models of Christian faith generally. The renunciations they demand are thus not mainly required for a particular ministry, but for common fidelity to the Gospel of the reign of God. This is precisely what the evangelists had in mind when they attributed these statements to Jesus.

The underlying cause of it all is the reign of God, that is, the imminent intervention of God in our history whereby he was going to impose his law of love, destroying all oppression and evil, thus inaugurating our salvation. The appointed time had arrived. The only thing left to do was to repent and accept the glad tidings. This was what Jesus hoped for and proclaimed. Of course, we do not know just how Jesus visualized the relationship between the painful present and the liberating future, because he, although he had such a lively and fresh imagination (as his parables abundantly demonstrate), nevertheless distinguished himself from the mainstream of the apocalyptic movement in his day, not only by putting the reign of God above all political violence and stressing the need to prepare ourselves to receive it, but also by his refusal to determine the time and manner of the final in-breaking of the mercy of God. Of course, if the resurrection of the just was going to take place soon, then family concerns would become extremely relative, since in that resurrection we would no longer marry or give in marriage, but would be like the angels in heaven (Mt 12:25). But Jesus did not tell us when this resurrection would take place, whether at the beginning or at the end of a process. The problem of an intermediate period during which people would continue marrying until everything culminated in the resurrection, as well as the duration of this intermediary period (if there was going to be one), was insoluble. Jesus was not concerned with it. What counted for him, and what the evangelists transmitted to us as his only message (Gospel), was the naked theological fact: God is going to save us. Although Jesus would remove a group of men and women from their homes to work with him, he did not intend to take those who accepted his message either out of the world or out of history, in order to create with them some visionary sect. He left them in their houses, with their families and their occupations. It is on this religious *datum*—that God is going to save us—that we must bring to bear the demands of the kingdom of God, as stated by Jesus.

DEMANDS OF CONVERSION

K. Berger, in *Die Gesetzauslegung Jesu,* has offered us a key for interpreting the accounts of the call to follow Jesus which, according to him, took shape in the Jewish-Hellenistic Church.[18] These narratives were modeled on the kind of stories of the conversion of Gentiles to Judaism that were popular among Hellenistic Jews. For the latter, the ideal paradigm of vocation-conversion was God's command to Abraham, to leave all things and become a pilgrim (Gen 12:1–9). The well-meaning Gentile, too, must abandon all things in order to enter into the promise. However, it is clear that the Hellenistic Jews did not demand that these proselytes actually break with their families or give up their possessions. They only meant to underscore the unique value of the covenant that God was offering them, in comparison with which all other relationships dwindled into insignificance, although remaining materially intact. Those Hellenistic Jews who were converted to Christianity applied this same model to Jews who continued in faithful observance of the law (Mt 19:21). These, too, had to be converted to the Gospel of Jesus. Jesus represented something entirely new, even in relationship to the Mosaic law, because the divine sovereignty which was to be revealed in the parousia had already revealed itself to be present in Jesus. Now, in comparison with the grace of God revealed in the resurrection of Jesus, everything else paled into insignificance. In fact, the first disciples, all of whom were Jews, are presented in the Synoptic tradition as models of conversion. As soon as Jesus issued his call to conversion, these men and women had followed him.

This interpretation of these accounts confirms us in our exegesis of the demands made in the sayings on the following of Jesus. Jesus states that no reality, even those as directly related to the creative work of God as family or earthly possessions (both of which appear in the original vocation of humankind in Genesis), and, indeed, even the desire to preserve one's own life, can be allowed to come between a person and the offer of the kingdom. It will not do to say: I am married (cf. Lk 14:20), or I have so many goods. Nor will it do to allow riches to take possession of our hearts, preventing us from responding to God's love. Nothing counts in comparison with this: the individual stands alone and naked in the face of the imminent reign of God. In fact, what Jesus was doing was simply to apply, in the context of the expectation in which he lived, the commandment to love God: ''Hear, O Israel: The Lord our God is one Lord; and you shall love the Lord your God with all your heart, and with all your soul . . .'' (Mk 12:29; Dt 6:4–5). To love God, in the experience of Israel, did not entail renouncing God's gifts, but only not allowing anything to take the place that belonged to God alone. No creature should be allowed to enter the sanctum where faith in God and love of him unfold. What is directly opposed to the first commandment is idolatry. Jesus translates this first commandment into the dynamic context of his own hope in the imminent reign of grace. He says, in effect: ''God is beginning to establish his reign, and you must allow nothing to hinder you from accepting it, whether family, possessions or even love for your own life.'' As regards the family, certain sayings attributed to Jesus echo the eschatological motif of divisions produced within the same family because of the great events of the end-time (cf. Mt 10:36; Lk 12:53).

By these demands, Jesus was not asking everyone who accepted his eschatological message to renounce their families or goods in a material sense, let alone by some public legal act, such as a bill of divorcement (!) or a transfer of goods. Nor was he even speaking about their being prepared for the possibility of having to do so out of fidelity to the kingdom, if worst came to worst and they had to make a choice. Rather, what he was asking for was a radical and total orientation of their own lives toward the reign of grace that was beginning, because this kingdom, which was so new and so opposed to present evil, would brook no rivals. This radical orientation would give them the strength to sacrifice everything for the kingdom, should family opposition or religious persecution come. And Jesus seems to have foreseen that such opposition and persecution would indeed come. He himself was experiencing it with increasing force.

And now, the same experience began to be felt by the first Christian communities. Adherence to the Gospel was bound to give rise to tensions within orthodox Jewish families. And when the disciples of Jesus were excommunicated by the religious authorities of Israel, they would be banned even from belonging to the beloved people. Then, even their family goods became an obstacle standing between those who were being persecuted and their Christian faith. It seems that the earliest churches had to insistently remind those who were in crisis of the sayings of the Lord and of the example of the first disciples, who left everything in order to follow Jesus. This was how the earliest churches came to understand both the Lord's sayings on following him and the accounts of the call of the disciples. It should be noted that the first communities of Christians neither imposed celibacy on anyone (the apostles—except Paul—the relatives of the Lord, and Peter all followed with their wives; cf 1 Cor 9:4–5), nor made the renunciation of goods obligatory (Acts 5:4).

TAKEN LITERALLY?

Recently, scholars have been underscoring the preponderant role played in primitive Christianity by itinerant prophets. Jesus, they remind us, exercised his prophetic ministry while traveling from place to place. He likewise sent his disciples to proclaim the good news by going from town to town within Israel and not, certainly, for the purpose of organizing stable, local communities. The latter would follow later, with the rise of the Church. But it is evident that the example of Jesus and the first disciples must have been closely followed, at least for some time. The Book of Acts shows that some of the seven ministers of the Jewish-Hellenistic group at Jerusalem became itinerant apostles (Acts 8:4; 11:19ff). Paul and Barnabas tirelessly made the rounds of the Christian communities of the diaspora, and it should be borne in mind that it was precisely these two who were distinguished by a rule of life that entailed going from place to place, unaccompanied by a wife, and working for a living (1 Cor 9:4–7).

Gerd Theissen has pointed out that while written texts maintain their original character, those transmitted orally tend to be modified to reflect the social conditions of the groups who preserve them.[19] Applying this to the case in point, we note that the sayings of the conditions for discipleship, which were transmitted orally for a period of roughly thirty years, reflect the bent of people who have no fixed abode and have left their families. These sayings correspond to the sort of radical attitude that we would expect of itinerant folk. For this very reason, according to Theissen, they must have been preserved by a group which, contrary to the common interpretation, took them literally as a rule of life. We know, in fact, that there were itinerant prophets in early Christianity and that some of them, according to the Didache, followed "the rules of the Lord."[20] E. Käsemann holds as certain the existence of a group of wandering charismatics among whom the Q document took shape.[21] The "mission rule" must have served as the norm of life for this group of Palestinian preachers. It is quite significant that all of the sayings on the following of Jesus that have come down to us have been preserved in the Q source, although Mark seems to have known only one of them in a secondary version (Mk 8:34, on carrying one's cross).

This hypothesis is very attractive. These prophets or evangelizers, who believed that the coming of the Son of Man was very near (indeed, he would come before they made the rounds of the towns of Israel; cf. Mt 10:23), would have left their families and despoiled themselves of all they possessed, out of a desire to prepare their fellow countrymen for the great end. They would have been the first, then, to adopt a quite literal interpretation of the sayings on discipleship and the accounts on the call of the disciples, at a period that was still very close to the lifetime of Jesus and still a long way off from that of the first anchorites. It should be noted, however, that they did so under the impulse of a vocation to an itinerant prophetic ministry, and that their attitude was based on an imminent expectation of the parousia. Their vision of reality was still of the kind that we referred to in the preceding chapter as dynamic eschatological dualism.

Moreover, we know—and this is not just an hypothesis, but an historically demonstrated fact—that these itinerant prophets continued to appear, not only throughout the Church, but particularly in Syria, one of the places where the monachate would later appear in greatest strength. Naturally, there would be considerable historical change in Christian milieus, and while the monks would flee to their solitude in hopes of a divine future (they wanted above all to be saved, thus anticipating an angelic life), the great world about them was beginning to feel the heavy influence of another type of dualism, of a static, spiritualistic sort. They, too, would take literally "the precepts of the Lord."

Notes

1. *Examen* 3,13.
2. *Examen,* 4, 1–2; *Constit.,* 3, 1,7.
3. RM, 87,13; 87,14; 87,39; 91,18; 91,44.
4. *Reg.* OFM, 1223, c. 2.
5. *Reg.* 2,4.
6. *Examen,* 4, 1–2; Constit. 3,1,7.
7. *Catechèse,* CSCO 160, 14, 17.20.
8. *Ep.* 2,2.
9. *Ep.* 125,20.
10. LG, 44.
11. PC, 1.
12. PC, 2.
13. PC, 5.
14. PC, 8.
15. PC, 2a.
16. LG, 40.
17. LG, 10, 15, 17, 25. Cf. LG, 42.
18. K. Berger, *Die Gesetzauslegung Jesu, 1: Markus und Parallelen* (Neukirchen, 1972) pp. 422–427.
19. G. Theissen, *"Wanderradikalismus, Literatursoziologische Aspekte des Uberlieferung von Worten Jesu im Urchristentum,"* ZThK 70 (1973) 245–271.
20. *Did.* XI,8.
21. E. Käsemann, "Zum Thema der urchristlichen Apokalyptik" in *Exegetische Versuche und Besinnungen* 2: 78–80, 115.

Bibliography

J.M. Lozano, *Discipleship. Towards an Understanding of Religious Life* (Chicago: CCRS, 1983) pp. 2–28.

T.F. O'Meara, *Holiness and Radicalism in Religious Life* (New York: Herder, 1970).

J.B. Metz, *Followers of Christ* (New York: Paulist, 1978) pp. 3–44.

Th. Matura, *Gospel Radicalism. The Hard Sayings of Jesus* (Maryknoll: Orbis, 1983).

F.J. Moloney, *Disciples and Prophets* (New York: Crossroad, 1981) pp. 133–154.

J.M.R. Tillard, *A Gospel Path, Religious Life* (Brussels: Lumen Vitae, 1975).

III | The Religious Life as a Parable

We cannot sidestep one fact that is, at first glance, clearly disconcerting. The fact is this: Not only primitive anchoritism (since the end of the third century), but also other forms of the religious life, such as those fostered by Basil and Macrina (fourth century) and later by Francis and Clare of Assisi (thirteenth century), were all born of a literal, and apparently naive, interpretation of certain Gospel texts. Antony, Hilarion and Cassian, as well as Francis of Assisi, would surely have been astounded if someone told them that Jesus had probably never asked anyone to make a material and radical renunciation of their goods, and that he did not expect this of his disciples as a general norm. The surprise of these holy men would even be greater if they were told that although Jesus chose celibacy for himself, he did not consider it an essential requisite for the expectation and proclamation of the kingdom of God, since the Gospel tradition itself shows that he chose almost every one of his disciples from among married people, and that although the following of Jesus in his prophetic ministry involved many difficulties for their family life, these disciples seem to have returned frequently to their families during most of the short period they spent together with him.

The case is further complicated when we consider that not only did Jesus himself not demand these kinds of material renunciations, but not even the evangelists had them in mind when they transmitted either the account of the calling of the disciples or the dominical sayings on the conditions for being associated with Jesus in the expectation and proclamation of the kingdom. What the Gospel texts are really asking for is not the abandonment of all things, but the unique value of the saving grace of God, in comparison with which everything else pales into insignificance on that deep, religious level where we make our most fundamental decisions. This applies even to the commandment to love God with all one's heart, which does not essentially entail adopting a life of celibacy.

The fact remains, however, that the monks, beginning with Antony at the end of the third century, took these Gospel sayings quite literally, and that they regarded them not as counsels, but as "precepts of the Lord," an expression that we find later in Basil and Benedict. Can we say, then, that the religious life was born of an erroneous interpretation of Scripture? We certainly know that the term "perfect" in Mt 19:21 was interpreted differently when it passed from the original Matthean sense into the Hellenistic world. In the First Gospel, "perfection" is the objective situation of those who *already* believe in Christ and follow him, come what may. In Origen, "perfection" means a subjective, moral state which can be attained only gradually, by means of the renunciation of all riches. But we do not know whether or not the first anchorites, many of whom did not know Greek, had assimilated this Hellenistic notion of perfection as a state of soul that had to be attained progressively. We do know, however, that the material renunciation of riches was considered by the Hellenistic philosophers of those times to be a necessary condition for anyone who wished to profess the life of a philosopher. Hellenistic schools of philosophy tended to be schools of spirituality, because they all taught people how to be truly human beings, and most of them purported to show their adepts the way they must follow in order to encounter the divinity. This environment certainly favored a literal interpretation of renunciation.

THE RELIGIOUS LIFE, A WORK OF THE SPIRIT

This attempt to explain the birth of the monachate mainly by attributing it to a mistaken interpretation of the literal sense of the Gospel texts on the conditions of discipleship, and of the message that the accounts of the call of some of the disciples meant to convey, is doomed to fail, for a number of reasons.

To begin with, we must never lose sight of the fact that the religious life and its various forms have, above all, an historical and ecclesial explanation. The monachate came into being as a development of the powerful ascetical movement that had been growing in the Church throughout the third century. At the same time, it seems to have arisen in response to a need in the Church. The complaints registered by Jerome and Basil against the clergy's assimilation of a worldly spirit are significant here. The possibility of martyrdom had ceased to act as a catalyst to community fervor. Anyone searching for a radical form of communion with Christ had to think of monastic asceticism. It is worth noting that Origen applied to the martyrs the same texts on the following of Jesus that the monks would use, a few decades later, in order to explain their way of life. Basil and Augustine, in the forms of life they fostered, under the influence of biblical and Hellenistic thought patterns, were striving to give intense expression to the kind of communion that Christian communities, dispersed throughout the Empire, were no longer able to express. In the same way, centuries later, the Mendicant Orders would continue the evolution begun by the *Pauperes Christi,* and would likewise be offering a response, through their image of the Church of the poor, to an urgent need of their times. For the moment, we will leave it at this, because it is clear that the apostolic institutes that began to appear from that time on could clearly justify their way of life in the needs of the Church and contemporary society.

If we set the fact of a *literal* reading of the Gospels or of Acts (Augustine) in their various historical contexts, we will observe how this literal reading was the occasion of a religious experience, which in turn set a religious movement in motion. To this day, no one has imagined that these singular forms of Christian life came into being as the result of some merely intellectual exercise. No one makes the decision to commit his or her whole life to an ideal at the end of some purely intellectual process. The decision to embrace the religious life is not the result of a theoretical interpretation, but rather of an inspiration, that is to say, of an interior impulse. Athanasius tells us that Antony felt personally challenged by Christ's words to the rich young man ''as if God himself had inspired him with the remembrance of the saints (the apostles), and as if the passage in the Gospel had been read for him.''[1]

Even more expressive, perhaps, is Francis of Assisi's reaction to the mission sermon. Overflowing with joy, the saint exclaimed: ''This is what I desire, this is what I am seeking, this is what I have been yearning for with all my heart!''[2] The project was already written in his heart, and the Gospel texts did no more than help Francis formulate it with greater clarity. That is exactly what happened: the spirit of these men and women was already oriented toward the religious life in one or another of its forms before they were aware of it. In the *Second Life,* Thomas of Celano coincides, in effect, with Athanasius, when he tells us that Francis and his companions, too, felt personally challenged by God in the reading of Scripture when, after opening the book three times at random, they successively encountered the following texts: Mt 19:21 ("If you would be perfect . . ."), Lk 9:3 ("Take nothing for your journey . . .") and Lk 9:23 ("If any man would come after me, let him deny himself . . .").[3] Anthony Claret, who discovered his apostolic vocation in reading certain texts from the prophets ("There were passages that impressed me so deeply that I seemed to hear a voice telling me the message I was reading"),[4] never claimed that these texts were speaking of him, or that they had that sense literally in the Bible. But even today, those of us who critically read the New Testament passages on the following of Christ that we have been referring to feel personally challenged and touched when we prayerfully consider how Jesus called Peter or how Mary Magdalene, filled with grateful love, followed Jesus.

Anyone who is aware of the fruits and the irradiative power of the religious life throughout the centuries can do no less than concur with Athanasius, Jerome and Thomas of Celano, when they state that it was God who called Antony, Hilarion and Francis. The same can be said of Anthony Claret, when he states that while reading the Bible, he felt called by the Spirit. It is the Holy Spirit who creates the religious life in the Church. And may we not say that the Spirit, like the tree in the Gospel, may be known by his fruits? Speaking from a slightly different angle, St. Paul states that there are some in the Church who receive a charism of celibacy, as he understands it, namely, to live a life of utter commitment to the Lord and his affairs. Now celibacy is precisely the fundamental charism of the religious life, the charism that creates it. And the charisms are gifts of the Spirit—in this case, vocational gifts—for the good of the Christian community.

The divine Spirit creates the religious life and its various forms (so we learn from history) by bringing to mind the remembrance of Jesus (the *memoria Jesu*) and of his total commitment to the kingdom of God, and by presenting the disciples who together with Jesus committed themselves to the expectation and proclamation of the kingdom, as a model

or source of inspiration to others. Naturally, the awareness of this vocation comes at the end of a latent period and in varying ways, because
God speaks to us in many ways. But very frequently, the discovery of a
calling to the religious life (which always culminates in prayer-response)
comes during a public or private reading of the Scriptures. The Spirit
uses the Gospel in order to summon up the awareness of a vocation.
When this happens, the holy book ceases being a text for critical anal-
ysis, and becomes a white-hot message. The Holy Spirit rereads it for
us and applies it to us. Quite understandably, the texts which arouse the
awareness of a vocation to the religious life are precisely those Gospel
accounts that deal with the call of the disciples of Christ and with the
immediate response (Mark) of those who are called. Or else the operative
texts are those which state the radical demands of the common Christian
vocation, because in the particular vocation to the religious life, candidates are faced with the same kinds of radical renunciations.

RELIGIOUS LIFE AND EVANGELICAL LIFE

But we believe that the connection between these Gospel texts on
discipleship and the religious life goes far deeper. This connection will
appear more clearly if we relate the religious life to the common Christian vocation.

Until recently, two fundamental reasons have generally been given
concerning the relation between the religious life and common Christian
life according to the Gospel. And both have used precisely those Gospel
sayings relating to the following of Christ, above all Mt 19:21 (''If you
would be perfect, sell . . . , give . . . , come, follow me'').

The first set of explanations is based precisely on the renunciations
entailed by these texts. From the fourth century until the beginning of
the twelfth, some Fathers and Doctors, following a Neoplatonic anthropology, taught that virginity was the original vocation of humankind. For
the Neoplatonists, human being is essentially pure spirit, imprisoned in
a body. Human beings are thus not *per se* corporeal, nor, consequently,
is sex something that belongs to their essence: it is an unfortunate cir-
cumstance that befalls them. The Fathers and Doctors saw a confirmation of this anthropology in the account in Genesis, where Adam and Eve
had sexual relations and procreated children *after* they had sinned. If
they had not sinned—so said these Fathers and Doctors—they would not

have had sexual relations and, at least according to Gregory of Nyssa, they would have increased and multiplied mentally, like angels. It was because of sin that men and women have to generate offspring as the animals do. From this point of view, the virgin and the celibate (thus, all monks and nuns) are the only ones who perpetuate the original vocation of humankind: they return to the condition of paradise. Most men and women, they add, do not have the strength for this, and thus they marry. They are, so to speak, children, "the weak." They will find salvation through the works of mercy, but they will be judged precisely by "the strong," namely, by those who were able to renounce marriage. This characterization of the laity as "the weak" who were incapable of renunciation, and of monks and nuns as "the strong," who could, is clearly stated in the works of Gregory the Great, Jonas of Orléans, Urban II (in 1092) and, for the last time, in the document whereby the papal legates (1125) confirmed the Premonstratensian Order.

If we apply these ideas to the problem we are discussing, it is quite clear that—within this perspective—monks and virgins are the only ones who live the Christian vocation in its totality. Christ himself, who was celibate for the sake of the kingdom of God, was the one who reactualized the original vocation of humankind to virginity, and it is under the aegis of his grace that virginity has again begun to flourish. Married Christians, on the contrary, are those who are incapable of living this vocation on earth. Those of them who dutifully practice the works of mercy will live that virginal vocation in heaven. We can conclude, from this line of thinking, that matrimony is not properly the object of a vocation, but rather something allowed by God's mercy for the weak.

This explanation was abandoned in the course of the twelfth century. Bear in mind that the last *official* text in which we find this explanation is from 1125. This explanation was abandoned because it no longer agreed with the world-view which was developing throughout the twelfth century, which was marked by a proto-Renaissance when thinkers again focused their attention on nature, when reason began to reclaim its rights in law and theology, and when what would come to be called natural and earthly values began to be accorded due consideration. Shortly afterward, Aristotelian influences would end the long sway of Neoplatonic anthropology, and human being would again be regarded as an essential composite of soul and body.

All of this had as its effect the full reincorporation of the layperson, whether man or woman, into spirituality. Before the middle of the twelfth century, the canon regular Gerhoh von Reichersberg (d. 1169) stated that lay Christians, too, renounce the world and its pomps, and that therefore every Christian, whether rich or poor, noble or serf, merchant or farmer, must live according to a rule of life based on Catholic faith and the teaching of the apostles.[5] Stephen of Muret, in his sermon on the basic unity of the different rules, stated that the fundamental rule for all Christians, whether laity, monks or canons, is the Gospel.[6] The Christian mind had not only discovered a common base for Christian spirituality, but also a means to avoid presenting lay Christians as second-class citizens. In the mainstream of the thirteenth century, Jacques de Vitry called all Christians "regulars," because (using an expression found in the Rule of the Master and in the Rule of Benedict) they serve the Lord under the same rule ("regula") of the Gospel, and under the supreme abbot, Christ.[7] By that time the Third Orders were coming into existence, and they made notable attempts to disseminate a truly evangelical spirituality among the laity.

THE STATE OF PERFECTION "TO BE ACQUIRED"

There was a need, then, throughout the thirteenth century, to have recourse to another explanation of the relation between the religious life and evangelical life, and this explanation was given by Scholasticism. During this time, too, the fundamental text used was Mt 19:21, with an accent on the initial words, "If you would be perfect," but understanding "perfection" (as Origen had in the third century) in the Hellenistic sense, as a subjective state which the individual achieves in relative fullness only through a gradual process. The abandonment of goods thus became a means of individual ascetical perfection which could be attained in time.

The new explanation consisted in the affirmation that the religious life is the state of perfection "to be acquired" *(status perfectionis acquirendae),* as opposed to the state of perfection "acquired" *(status perfectionis acquisitae),* which is proper of bishops. All of us, certainly (as St. Thomas Aquinas reminds us), are called to Christian perfection, because this perfection consists in none other than the fullness of love to which the Lord's first commandment calls us. But a necessary prerequisite for any state, and thus for a state of perfection, is a permanent commitment made with some solemnity and, in the case in point, a commitment to those matters relating to perfection.[8] Religious do this when they commit themselves to abstain from secular realities, even though the latter are lawful in themselves, in order to attain the perfection of union with God through love.[9] The "evangelical counsels," that is, celibacy, poverty and obedience, are, for St. Thomas, means and instruments of perfection.

The argument of St. Thomas can be understood in two ways. First, in the sense that only the religious makes a public commitment to tend toward the perfection of love. He seems to be saying this, for example, when he compares the religious life with the life of secular priests.[10] Understood in this sense, we would find it hard to assent to the Thomist thesis today, because the commitment to tend toward perfection seems to us to be entailed in the reception of baptism and confirmation, and thus in the very basis of Christian life from which the various kinds of Christian life take their starting point. This seems equally clear to us in the sacramental celebration of matrimony, especially if the latter is viewed not merely as a legitimation of a pure love that comes from the Creator, but much more as an affirmation made before the Church of the Christian reality of this love and as a commitment of the married couple to help each other in being disciples of Jesus. Besides this, although not on the level of acts that give rise to a kind of life, the commitment to tend toward the fullness of love is implicitly present whenever we approach the sacrament of reconciliation or celebrate the Eucharist.

If, however, we understand the Thomistic argument in the more cautious sense that only religious are committed to the "counsels" of celibacy, poverty and obedience, as instruments of perfection, we must still make a few observations. In the first place, we would observe that both Jesus and his disciples adopted an uprooted style of life (although the latter did not materially renounce their goods, and most of them did not embrace celibacy), in order to commit themselves to the proclamation of the kingdom of God. Moreover, St. Paul understands celibacy not just as an exclusive relationship of love with the Lord, but also as freedom to give oneself to the affairs of the Lord and of his Church (1 Cor 7:32), basing this on his own experience (2 Cor 11:23–29; cf. 1 Cor 9:4–7). St. Thomas, in contrast, moves within a perspective of individual perfection. In the second place, this theory is connected with the opinion according to which, as St. Thomas himself states, those in the religious life keep the counsels, whereas those in the secular life keep only the commandments—a vision of moral theology that few would accept today. But even leaving aside for a moment the question of the "counsels," one would have to ask, in the third place, whether one may exclusively single out the religious life as a state of perfection by the mere fact that it entails the renunciation of secular realities that might hinder the pursuit of perfect love, since all Christians commit themselves to tend toward the perfection of the Christian life that has been infused in us through baptism and renewed each time we take part in the other sacraments. After all, are not the sacraments active instruments for growth in faith, hope and love and, by that very fact, more direct means to perfection than those which consist merely in removing obstacles to perfection?

At any rate, it is a fact that the Second Vatican Council abandoned the expression "state of perfection" to designate the religious life in the documents that deal expressly with the latter. The expression had been introduced into the Constitution on the Liturgy on two occasions, in reference to those "institutes of the state of perfection" that recite the whole or part of the Liturgy of the Hours.[12] But when the discussion later turned to the meaning of the religious life for the Church, this expression was carefully avoided, to the point that the Council refused to entitle Chapter VI of *Lumen Gentium* "The Members of Institutes of the State of Perfection," which some of the fathers had proposed, and opted instead to call it "Religious," despite the fact that this would apparently exclude the members of secular institutes. These texts—so it was explained in full council session—referred also to secular institutes in matters in which they and religious Institutes coincide, but the council declined the suggestion to use the expression "institutes of states of perfection," although it had been used recently to refer jointly to both types of Institutes. And, finally, let it be noted that the new Code of Canon Law has also laid aside the expression "state of perfection."

TOWARD A NEW VISION

After the council, then, we seemed to be left without a systematic interpretation of the relationship between the religious life and other forms of following Christ. On the one hand, of course, it was not the council's task to give us a technical explanation, but, on the other, the theology of the religious life did not really begin to flourish again until theologians were invited by the council to offer their contribution. The importance accorded to the common vocation to evangelical perfection, the express and insistent extension of the following of Christ to all Christians, and the Church's new sensibility to the "world" all contributed to a global vision of Christian vocation in which religious would have to look for a place to fit. The council helped us, not by giving us a theology, but by providing us with a set of fundamental concepts. It would be up to the experts to see how these doctrinal elements had to be combined and how the various tendencies had to be unified. It is quite clear, for example, that Chapter VI of *Lumen Gentium* offers us a more monastic vision of the religious life than does *Perfectae Caritatis.*

The fact that the drafters of the new Code of Canon Law for the Latin Church chose the phrase "institutes of consecrated life" as the common title for that part of the Code relating both to religious and to secular Institutes might suggest that they were working out of a theological vision starting from the concept of consecration to God. This is practically the same vision as that of St. Thomas, who starts from the act of committing oneself to the service of God, in order to develop his doctrine on the religious life. But the concept of consecration needs to be well defined, so as to give it a precise biblical and theological meaning, derived not from the concept of the sacred in primitive religions, but from the very experience of Jesus.

From yet another viewpoint, this special self-gift to the service of God has be understood as association with Christ Jesus; moreover, the Gospel texts relating to communion with the Lord have evoked and created this deep sense and state of association. The following of Jesus is not only fundamental in the Gospel description of Christian existence; it has also been the creative inspiration of the religious life. Here we find the unequivocally Christian roots of Christian religious life, and not just some common base for any form of monasticism, whether Christian or not. It is in Jesus that we have encountered the Father, and it is his example that has moved us to commit ourselves to serving the kingdom of God. It would not be out of place to point out here that the Second Vatican Council, in the decree *Perfectae Caritatis,* has taken the concept of the following of Christ as the point of departure for its way of viewing the religious life, thereby giving us a more dynamic vision of that life. The presentation of the religious life as a fact in the Church begins with

"those men and women who determined to follow Christ . . ."[13] The
supreme norm of religious living is "the following of Christ."[14] The
renunciations involved in the religious life are a participation in the *kenosis* of Christ, and religious profession means leaving all things for
Christ's sake, regarding him as the one thing necessary.[15] Poverty is
practiced in the following of Christ[16] and obedience is a communion with
Christ in his pursuit of God's will.[17]

During the years of the council and since then, theologians have laid
considerable stress on expressly connecting the religious life with our
common Christian roots. They have also frequently spoken of "evangelical life." And indeed the whole *raison d'être* of Christian religious
existence is the Gospel. In this connection, various writers have cited St.
Basil who, in his catechism for an evangelical brotherhood, speaks of
this type of life as the "faithful observance of the Gospel." But Basil
apparently did not know how to relate this particular type of life—in celibacy and in community—with the common Christian vocation. Must we
not also say that the life of a Christian in the world is also evangelical?
Recall that for some of the Fathers and throughout a good part of the
Middle Ages, celibacy was regarded as the only Christian vocation properly so-called, and only those who renounced their goods were considered to be living the Gospel in its fullness. This way of looking at things
has been set aside by the Church and is thus untenable today. There has
also been a good deal of talk about "evangelical radicalism." Religious
are said to give a radical interpretation of the Gospel through their lives.
And this is also true, although it needs to be said just how it is true. But
we must by all means avoid giving the impression that we regard the life
of lay Christians living in the world as a sort of halfway or half-hearted
approach to the Gospel (especially in the way St. Gregory the Great defined the life of the laity as a "yes and no" to the Gospel).

RELIGIOUS LIFE AND PROPHECY

The religious life, then, comes into existence because certain men
and women, disciples of Jesus, have felt moved by the Spirit to embrace
a kind of life that takes—in their material and literal sense—the accounts
of the call of the first disciples and the dominical sayings on the demands
of the following of Christ. These accounts and sayings (as we are weary
of repeating) were not meant to be construed materially, and therefore

do not constitute counsels or recommendations of the Lord for those "who would be perfect," but, rather, are basic principles of fidelity to the kingdom for all. They are reformulations, in eschatological terms, of the first commandment of love. What relationship is there, then, between the religious life and the evangelical life which has as its norms these sayings on the following of Christ? It is our personal belief that the relationship between them is the same as the one that unites prophecy to reality.

Some of the close relationships between what we have come to call the religious life and prophecy have lately been coming to the fore. In the first place, the sayings on the conditions for following Jesus referred originally to those men and women who accompanied him and collaborated with him in his prophetic ministry. Like Jesus, the disciples left all to commit themselves to the proclamation of the kingdom of God and to make this kingdom visible through the healings they performed. It is quite possible that the account of the vocation of Elisha was the inspiration for the Gospel accounts of the call of the first disciples and, at any rate, the latter were closer to the followers of the prophet John the Baptist than they were to the followers of the rabbis. Later, those who followed the "precepts of the Lord" would mainly be prophets. Jesus and his disciples left their families and occupations because God was beginning to manifest himself definitively in history to save his people. Not only in their preaching and healing ministries, but even more deeply in their very lives, God's future began to shine through. Their persons, their lives, their words and actions, were in themselves a prophetic interpretation of history, in the sense that they disclosed the incipient presence of God in history and prepared the present for the future of grace. One of Jesus' sayings, preserved by Matthew alone, concerning those who make themselves eunuchs for the sake of the kingdom, addresses itself precisely to this in-breaking of grace into the present, to such an extent that it deeply and radically modifies human existence. All of the demands that Jesus makes on his disciples (which would later be materially actualized in the religious life) draw their sole reason for being from the in-breaking of God's kingdom into history and, for that same reason, proclaim it. Originally, these demands of Jesus were united to the prophetic ministry— and on a deep level, because these demands presupposed accepting the message of Jesus fully and, in some cases because they were closely connected with the prophetic type of life followed by Jesus.

In actualizing these demands literally, the religious life has in some way kept their original, prophetic thrust. In the following chapter, we shall see how the religious life and its various forms have come and still come into existence, by basing themselves on a spiritual reading of history and as a response to certain emerging situations. The response has always entailed a transcending of the present situation by confronting it with God, his word and his grace. And this is, precisely, prophecy.

This is what Vatican II refers to when it speaks of the religious life as "a sign which can and should effectively inspire all the members of the Church to unflaggingly fulfill the duties of their Christian calling. For the people of God has here no lasting city but seeks the city which is to come, and the religious state of life, in bestowing greater freedom from the cares of earthly existence on those who follow it, simultaneously reveals more clearly to all believers the heavenly goods which are already present in this age, witnessing to the new and eternal life which we have acquired through the redemptive work of Christ and preluding our future resurrection and the glory of the heavenly kingdom."[18]

SIGNS AND PARABLES

The Second Vatican Council used a typically prophetic term when it defined the religious life as a sign of the divine transcendence. In the Bible, a "sign" is a prophet's action (and not necessarily a miraculous one) which contains a divine message. Among such non-oracular signs we might mention Isaiah's imposing a heavy name on one of his sons (Is 8:1–4), or his walking about naked and barefoot for three years (Is 20:1–6). Other instances would be Ezekiel's engraving the portrait of a besieged city on a brick (Ez 4:1–3), or his lying on his left side for three hundred and ninety days, and on his right side for another forty days (Ez 4:4–7). Although the word "sign" is not used, it is clear that another instance in this category was Jeremiah's remaining single, to indicate that there was no future for his people (Jer 16:1–4). In this last case, it should be noted, we are dealing not with an action, but with a type of life. In Lk 11:29–32 (and implicitly in Mt 12:39–40), one Old Testament personage, Jonah, is transformed into a sign. It should be noted that human actions and an individual's kind of life are transformed into signs, because God orders them or gives them their sign-meaning. Jonah was transformed into a sign by the will of God. It was God who gave this transcendent meaning to a human reality. This is exactly what happens in the kind of life we are concerned with here. The religious life is a sign in this sense—indeed, it is a sign for the whole Church. It becomes a sign because God calls it forth and because his love gives it meaning.

In fact, instead of the notion of sign, we might with equal or better right use the typically evangelical term "parable." Jesus made abundant use of parables, above all to proclaim the kingdom of God and to confront human beings with it. It has been shown that the rabbis used parables as pedagogical tools to explain some point of the law or of their teachings, whereas in Jesus' teaching they were not just an additional embellishment, but the very substance of his preaching. He proclaimed the kingdom of God and confronted his listeners with it through his parables. His parables were, then, metaphors—poetic uses of language taken from nature or from everyday experience, which surprised Jesus' listeners by their vividness or strangeness, thus piquing the interest of the crowd gathered around him. Jesus used this poetic language because his aim was not to offer a rational explanation of the kingdom of God, but to bring his listeners face to face with it. His audience grasped the reality of the in-breaking of this final grace by entering into the same situation of hope in which Jesus himself lived, spoke and acted.

We may go so far as to say that the genre of the parable does not seem to be limited to oral language. On occasions, the actions of Jesus themselves become parables. Once, for example, when he was addressing a group who seemed to think that the kingdom was something they could use to their own advantage, or in which they had some special privileges, Jesus took a little child, put him in their midst, and invited them all to become like this little child. He also washed their feet, to show them that in the kingdom, paradoxically, leading is serving. These gestures are certainly formative and hence pedagogical, but at the same time they challenge, invite and surprise us, as parables do. Expanding on this concept, we may say that there are even parabolic kinds of life. In the history of Israel prior to Jesus, the bachelorhood of Jeremiah was in itself a metaphorical message. Even before, Hosea's marriage to an unfaithful wife was in itself a challenging proclamation. The very life of Jesus during his ministry—his uprooted lifestyle, his leaving of family and livelihood in order to form a family of those who did the will of God—is in itself a parable. Through the veiled language of his own life, he spoke to his contemporaries about God and his saving love. Later, the life of his disciples would become, for the Church, a message, and not so much a didactic message (although it was that, too) as a call to face up to the presence of God in Jesus, although all the material details in the accounts of the disciples' life and calling did not have to be taken literally.

THE RELIGIOUS LIFE AS A PARABLE

This is exactly the meaning of the religious life in the Church. In order to remind the whole Church of the demands that the Gospel makes on us all (we must deny ourselves, take up the cross, rise above family ties, and not allow our concern for power, security and a life of ease to become our ultimate norm), the Spirit of the Lord Jesus calls a minority of men and women to renounce, materially and radically, their own families (both those they have left and those they might form themselves) and the whole search for personal power and security. Their family will be the Church (solitaries) or a particular group of disciples who jointly seek the will of God and declare their solidarity with the outcast and the oppressed, as Jesus did. Their public profession will in one way or another be the service of the Gospel. They will live exclusively in order to irradiate the faith and hope of Jesus and to proclaim his liberating message. Significantly, these particular vocations of a prophetic minority frequently arise from contact with those Gospel texts that set forth the demands of the kingdom of God before all Christians.

But neither do religious themselves pretend that their kind of life be taken according to the letter. It used to be said repeatedly that all Christians were called to live the spirit of the counsels, but not the counsels themselves in the material sense. And there was a strong element of truth in this, because the spirit, the content of this kind of life, is none other than the Gospel of the kingdom and its demands for all who seek the kingdom. We are dealing, then, with a kind of life, a type of Christian existence, which derives its meaning from the fact that it makes visible to the majority of the members of the Church the message of Jesus concerning the sovereignty and compassionate love of the Father. The religious life, as a life, does this by constantly bringing before the Church the *memoria Jesu et discipulorum*, the remembrance of the commitment of Jesus, and, with him, that of his disciples, to the reign of God. This is its essential function in the Church. It is a parable and, like every one of Jesus' parables, its content is the kingdom of God.

AN ASSESSMENT OF OTHER INTERPRETATIONS

Toward the end of our first chapter, we suggested that the principle established by Vatican II[19]—that the religious life must return to the sources of all Christian life and must therefore take the following of Christ as its supreme norm—must be applied not only to the practice but also to the very theological interpretation of, the religious life. For this reason, in Chapter II, we fixed our attention on Jesus, in whom it all began. This led us, in turn, to the conclusion that the religious life in its source (Jesus), in its models (the disciples) and in the first Christians who followed it (the itinerant prophets of the apostolic Church, and Paul) has a prophetic meaning and thrust. This led us, finally, to define the religious life as a living parable or a parabolic life of the kingdom of God.

Since the time of St. Basil and above all in recent times, there have been those who single out in the religious life its evangelical character. But as we have seen, the religious life is really no more evangelical than secular Christian life, because the Gospel speaks to us of faith, hope, conversion, purity of heart, humility, service and solidarity with the oppressed—and none of these are more related to the religious life than they are to secular Christian life. The religious life can be called evangelical only in the sense that, thanks to celibacy, it is a type of life created by the Gospel itself, and not simply taken over by the Gospel, as in the case of Christian matrimony.

Recently, too, there has been a tendency to view the religious life above all in terms of its evangelical radicalism. But we have already sufficiently shown that the radical demands of commitment to the kingdom of God by following Jesus are addressed, in the Gospels, to all Christians. No one can imagine that those whom God has called to matrimony or to other forms of Christian secular existence are dispensed from those demands. The relationship of the religious life to the radical demands of the Gospel consists precisely in the fact that—precisely as a type of Christian life—it is called to reveal them to the rest of the Church. It does not mean that religious commit themselves more to these demands than do lay Christians. Again we come to the conclusion that the distinctiveness of the religious life lies in its character as a prophetic message and as a parabolic statement.

The same can be said, in another manner, of the description of religious as men and women of the Absolute. We suspect that, behind this way of speaking, there lurks anew the ancient prejudice which viewed monks as total Christians and laypersons as halfway Christians. This becomes all the more clear when proponents of this approach interpret secular life as a sort of compromise. But one must strenuously object to this interpretation, because a layperson who is called by God to the married, single or widowed life as a way of traveling toward him (God is the Absolute) is surely not called to a life of compromise or of halfway measures. One gives oneself totally to God through secular realities. If one does not do so, then one is as unfaithful to one's vocation as a religious would be in a different set of circumstances. Religious as well as laypersons are such, because God has touched them absolutely and has consecrated them to his reign. We can see only one point of particular relationship between the religious life and commitment to the Absolute, and that has to do with the element of *exclusiveness* that characterizes the religious life, whereby that life becomes a manifestation of the absolute and unconditional love of God. Here again, then, we are brought back to the prophetic origins of the religious life.

Notes

1. *VA*, 2. Cf. Athanasius, *The Life of Anthony* (New York: Paulist, 1980) p. 31.

2. T. Celano, *Vita Prima*, c. 9. in S. Francis of Assisi, *Writings and Early Biographies* (Chicago: Franciscan Herald, 1973) p. 257.

3. *Vita Secunda*, I, c. 10. Ibid. p. 248.

4. *Autob.*, 114, cf. 113–120 (Chicago: Claretian Publications, 1973) pp. 48–50.

5. *De aedif. Dei*, c. 43: PL 194, 1302.

6. *Sermo de unitate diversarum regularum*, in Martene, *De antiquis Ecclesiae ritibus*, IV. Venetiis, 1783, p. 308.

7. *Libri duo, quorum prior Orientalis* . . . Duoai, 1597, p. 357.

8. 2-2 q 184 a 4.

9. 2-2 q 184 a 5.

10. 2-2 q 184 a 8.
11. *Quodl.* 4 a 23, s.c.4.
12. SC, 98, 101.
13. PC, 1.
14. PC, 2.
15. PC, 5.
16. PC, 13.
17. PC, 14.
18. LG, 44.
19. PC, 2.

Bibliography

A. Cussianovich, *Religious Life and the Poor* (Maryknoll: Orbis, 1979) pp. 21–33.
J.M. Lozano, *Discipleship: Toward an Understanding of Religious Life* (Chicago: CCRS, 1983) pp. 29–31.
L.M. Orsy, *Open to the Spirit* (Denville: Dimension Books, 1968) pp. 13–70.
The Prophetic Role of Religious. Donum Dei 23 (Ottawa: Canadian Religious Conference, 1977).
J.M.R. Tillard, *The Mystery of Religious Life* (Saint Louis: Herder, 1967) pp. 39–100.

IV   In the Service of the Reign of God

By now it should be sufficiently clear that the religious life is in itself a type of Christian life which has been brought into being by faith and hope in the reign of God, and which, therefore, functions as a sort of lived parable that allows other human beings to confront that reign, so to speak, in the flesh. It now remains for us to clarify something we have thus far been taking for granted, namely, the meaning of the reign of God and the implications, for the religious life and for the Church, of putting oneself in the service of the reign of God.

JESUS AND THE REIGN OF GOD

Jesus appeared above all as the decisive prophet of the reign or kingdom of God. In his day, his own people, Israel, had become a people of hope. The situation of political oppression—with strong religious overtones—in which his compatriots lived had led them to hope in some great, liberating action by God. This eagerly-awaited divine action was conceived of in various forms, and suggested correspondingly different ways of reacting to it, ranging from political struggle (the Zealots), to quasi-monastic separation from the rest of the community (Qumran), to conversion and penitential baptism (John the Baptist), to a rigorous observance of the law (the Pharisees). Apocalyptic writers unfolded, in figurative language, their dreams of the fall of the Roman oppressors. Jesus spoke of this longed-for divine action under the ancient symbol of the reign of God, to the extent of making this symbol not only the central, but practically the only theme of his preaching. While his hope in this kingdom and the tension his message set up between the present and the divine future (successive eschatological dualism) brought him close to apocalyptic currents of thought, Jesus was distinguished from them by his careful avoidance of any attempt to specify the manner or time of this great grace. Moreover, Jesus seems to have omitted one of the aspects commonly associated with the kingdom in popular expectations. According to these common expectations, the kingdom would have to be a grace reserved for the elect (whether the elect were thought of as Israel, the holy community of Qumran, or the strict observers of the law) and a definitive chastisement of the wicked (whether these were conceived of as the Gentile oppressors, the priests who had betrayed the holiness of the temple, or sinful non-observers of the law). For Jesus, the reign of God meant that God was about to impose his dominion, although the prophet from Nazareth seems to have presented this reign exclusively in terms of merciful and saving grace. For this reason, he preached this reign or kingdom to the lost sheep of Israel, he unconditionally proclaimed forgiveness to sinners, he had table fellowship with tax collectors and with people of ill repute, and he showed a fine sensibility toward women, whom the rabbis judged unworthy of learning the torah. He invited all to the banquet of God's abundant grace, beginning with the outcasts. His frequent banquets with the latter were in the nature of parabolic actions.

But there was more to it than that. For Jesus, the kingdom was certainly in the divine future and would culminate in it, but he felt and proclaimed it as something that was beginning now, humbly and quietly, in his ministry, in his healings and, implicitly, in his own person. The kingdom, then, is something that begins here and now, giving us a lively sense of urgency, until the fullness of grace will at length come. One must enter into the logic of this love of God for his sons and daughters, by a conversion leading to a change of life. One must be ready to rise above all else, in order to be ready to receive this wonderful kingdom. Hence, it is humanly impossible for the rich, who possess so much and are possessed by their possessions, to enter into the logic of this unique love of God. When Jesus was crucified and lifted up in glory, his disciples would understand that the definitive grace of salvation had been given us precisely in the cross and resurrection of Christ the Lord, although this grace will culminate only in our future communion with God in glory.

THE RELIGIOUS LIFE AND THE KINGDOM

Now it is easier for us to understand what it means for the religious life to be a sign and parable (a metaphoric message) of the reign of God. The religious life is called to reveal here and now the incipient presence of the reign of God, by pointing toward its definitive culmination in the glory of God. Jesus spoke of the kingdom as the very reason for which all of us must adopt a spiritual attitude of poverty, and for which some of us, like him, become eunuchs for the kingdom. This has often been understood in a rather inexact manner, as if the relationship between celibacy and the kingdom consisted in celibates' anticipating the general state of future glory when no one will marry or give in marriage. Indeed, none will marry, but neither will they be bachelors or spinsters, since that would suppose renunciations of a sort, and there is no place in glory for renunciations. Both matrimony and the single life are things of this world. What Jesus meant is that some persons have been so deeply touched by the experience of God's love (the saving love with which God loves them and their neighbors) that they no longer allow themselves to be governed by dreams of power or of the easy life, and can give up marriage in order to devote themselves exclusively to the experience of that love and to irradiating it. What the religious life truly reveals is the transcendent power of divine love.

The whole reason for being of the religious life does not lie in fleeing from the world or denying or escaping from it, but in revealing the presence, in the world, of the God who loves with infinite mercy, heals, pardons and saves. The religious life does this by being present in the world and at the same time transcending it, precisely through a kind of life whose wellspring is that saving love of God. If the religious life is to have that prophetic meaning that Jesus gave to his ministry and his life, it cannot consist in an escape from history, but, rather, in a bringing of the world and its history to God. Presence and transcendence are equally necessary.

Our way of viewing the intertwined relationships among the religious life, the reign of divine grace, and the world into which this kingdom is always in-breaking might come as a surprise to those who have often heard and read that, in the primitive monastic tradition, the great solitaries fled into the wilderness simply to attain their own eternal salvation. According to not a few of the desert sayings, they answered the burning question "How shall I be saved?" by embracing a life of solitude. In our introductory chapter, we already noted that this was not the motive most generally claimed throughout the history of the religious life, but we must admit that it played a preponderant role in the vocation of large numbers of anchorites. We must also point out that for many centuries the Church was largely unaware of the great fruitfulness of the contemplative life. It was often said that the so-called active life was useful to the Church, while the ease and rest of the contemplative life was useful only to those who practiced it. This point of view is amply documented in the Fathers. In this connection, it is interesting to note that the monks themselves shared something of this view. For example, when bishops were looking for monks to ordain as presbyters of their own communities, the latter excused themselves, not on the score that they were already useful to the Church because of their intercession, but rather on the grounds that, being unsure of their own salvation, they hardly felt capable of attending to the salvation of others. Clearly, a collective vision of the kingdom of God had been lost by being interpreted purely in terms of personal salvation. Evagrius of Pontus (d. 399), one of the great theologians of primitive monasticism, defines the reign of God as a mystical experience. The kingdom had become totally interiorized by being confined within the limits of individual experience.

It might be well in this context to recall a hermeneutical principle recently inculcated by the School of Konstanz: an historical fact does not derive its significance merely from the intention of those who produce it, but from the way in which this fact is received by society. Historical facts, to the extent that they are such, tend to change the prevailing situation and create new horizons not intentionally foreseen by the people who initiate them. The historical significance of these facts, then, ultimately depends on the reception they are given. This is exactly what happened with a fact of such importance for the Church as monasticism undoubtedly was. In order to assure their personal salvation, the primitive monks went into solitude and began to cultivate a life of asceticism and constant prayer. The Church, however, immediately called them servants of God, seeing in their lives something that went beyond their merely individual quest for salvation. Since the monks aimed at being always in the presence of God, their life was also called the angelic life (what we all hope to be, they would strive to attain in some way here and now), or, as it was said, they were attempting a return to paradise lost. Then prominent Church-figures began writing the lives of the most famous monks (the life of Antony became a best-seller), and these lives had a broad and deep impact on the whole Church. Thus, the life of monks and nuns took on a fully ecclesial and communitarian significance.

PROCLAMATION

By the fact that it is devoted to serving the kingdom of God in this world, the religious life is called to exercise a twofold function. The first aspect of this function consists of the proclamation of the ever-active presence of God in history to save us. This leads those in the religious life as such to embrace celibacy, solitude or community, and to embody common evangelical poverty in a public act, radically renouncing their own power and security. These commitments reveal the presence of grace first of all by their positive character. Celibacy for the sake of the kingdom amounts to a statement that the love of God (both in the active and the passive sense) is reason enough to live on. It always conveys the message that in a relationship of faith, hope and love with God, and in response to the love which God has first shown us, we find full meaning for our own lives. But the active and passive love of God can never be lived apart from the love whereby God loves all his sons and daughters and whereby every Christian must also love them. And, at least in the vast majority of cases, it is clear that a sane person is not going to embrace celibacy in the abstract. Some persons may embrace it in order to live a life of fuller intercession, while most persons do so in order to devote themselves more freely to the apostolate or to the loving works of mercy. These specific elements of the various forms of religious life are also part of their proclamation. By committing themselves to the care of the poor, religious are not solely or mainly testifying to their own love, but above all to the love whereby God shows a preferential care for the outcast and for the suffering. Even a purely contemplative life testifies to the personal, faith-filled relationship in lived prayer, which all Christians are called to foster. But a Christian contemplative life cannot help reflecting the love of our neighbor. For example, Carmelite contemplation (as in Teresa of Jesus and Thérèse of Lisieux) is also essentially intercession. In the depths of God, the monk or nun rediscovers the world that he or she has apparently abandoned.

Moreover, this proclamation is also effected by the negative aspects of this type of Christian life, namely, the renunciations which give the religious life its distinctive stamp: the foregoing of married and parental love, of the quest for personal power, of the ability to freely arrange the course of one's life. Both the positive aspects (love of God and neighbor) and the negative aspects (spousal and parental love) form a seamless unity.

THE "POOR" AND THE REIGN OF LOVE

Poverty has left a deep imprint on the religious life since its origins. Later we will examine just how deeply, but for the moment we need only say that, from the very beginnings of Christian monasticism, poverty has figured in two important and closely related ways. On the one hand, the act of renouncing one's property was the equivalent of what would later be called the act of profession. By this act the anchorites alienated themselves from the world, declaring their aloofness from the quest for power, security and ease into which the Church seemed to be lapsing. On the other hand, when they renounced their goods, they distributed them to the poor. Later, many solitaries would often distribute what they themselves did not need among the truly needy. The act of renunciation has been kept in all succeeding forms of religious life as the first step to be taken in the life of commitment to the service of God. When the first bourgeoisie of merchants and bankers began to discover the overwhelming power of money, the mendicant orders opted decisively to put themselves on the side of the poor. And numerous apostolic institutes have been founded precisely for the service of the poor. In our own century, the Little Sisters and Brothers of Jesus have returned to a life of quiet presence and communion among the marginated. And the religious life in the so-called third world has made communion with the poor its central focus.

All of the foregoing cases are little more than a reflection of the ministry and spirituality of Jesus. For him, the in-breaking of the kingdom meant the cessation of all suffering: the sick were healed, the poor received the glad tidings of their liberation, and the outcasts sat down at table with Jesus. And it is here, amidst poverty, discrimination and suffering, that the kingdom of divine grace shows all its power and where it takes root as an alternative to the present. The kingdom, which is always to come and never fulfilled in time, acts not so much like a "utopia" as it does like a powerful force inspiring countless individuals to commit themselves to it and calling a great number of activities into being.

It should be noted here that it was in the death and resurrection of Jesus, more than in his ministry, that the connection between the kingdom and poverty was most powerfully revealed, because Jesus, the prophet of the kingdom (into which tax collectors and prostitutes were entering ahead of the observant), went to his death as a man rejected and excommunicated. He was excommunicated by the priestly leaders of his people, who handed him over to the empire, which was for them the very symbol of the evil one. He was the lawbreaker par excellence, on whom, it seemed, the biblical curse had fallen. As he died, Matthew tells us, the veil of the temple was torn in two, revealing—we would add—a now-empty room. The God whom the priests and theologians thought they could control was with Jesus, in Jesus. And the Father raised him up. In his death and glorification, God began to establish his kingdom.

CRITICISM OF THE PRESENT

The proclamation of the future kingdom brings with it a criticism of the present order of things. For this reason the religious life, too, inasmuch as it is a lived parable of the kingdom, exercises a critical function, not only as regards civil society, but as regards the Church itself. This, we believe, is the fundamental meaning of what the first monks termed their *fuga mundi* (flight from the world, i.e., from the worldly compromises of the Church). Perhaps it might more accurately have been called their "critical presence in the world," judging from the influence of monasticism on society. This is above all true of the attitude of the later mendicant and apostolic institutes, which took a stand against those things in civil society or in the Christian community that were contrary to the Gospel: the loss of the sense of God, the worship of power as the supreme norm to which solidarity is sacrificed, the rampant growth and spread of selfishness. It suffices, without entering into details, to recall that the various forms of religious life have always come into being as a critical response to the ills of society and of the Church: primitive monasticism versus the growing worldliness of the clergy and the faithful; mendicants versus the nascent bourgeois ideal of profit over all; the Carmelite reform versus a power-drunk Spain and a divided Church; congregations devoted to the abandoned versus industrial capitalism. When the first Sisters of Adoration undertook the rehabilitation of prostitutes, they were not only showing their love for those whom Christ mercifully loved, but were also registering a protest against the condition of women in the nineteenth century. When a Little Sister of the Poor welcomes the elderly poor into her house, she is also making a critical statement against the way in which society and other Christians neglect or abandon the elderly.

In presenting these last examples, we are aware that we have passed from a form of criticism implicit in the very tenor of a particular kind of life, to one that is expressed in actions, but this does not break the thread of our logic. This is so, in the first place, because celibacy professed out of love for the Lord and out of a desire to be more fully committed to his concerns (1 Cor 7:32) finds its very meaning in acts of love, and, in the second place, because the women referred to in our examples have embraced celibacy precisely in order to be able to deal with those excluded by society. The following of Christ does not take place in the abstract or in a vacuum. We must always be bringing the remembrance of Jesus into our present.

It should be noted, however, that criticism can be a two-edged sword. In the first place, a reactionary mind-set may tend to expand this attitude of rejecting the world even to the extent of denying the positive values of religious life and its presence in the world. This may even lead us to forget that God's love for the world is more powerful than our desire to reject it, or else it may involve a total loss of a positive attitude toward the genuine values of society, leaving us trapped in a sterile, self-centered mentality. In the second place, religious must always keep their eyes open to the possible uses which the pagan spirit may attempt to make of their ministry to the poor. It is sobering to think of the misuses to which the pagan-controlled media can put the work of a holy religious who gathers up society's refuse, with apparent unconcern over the fact that society continues to cast its refuse into the streets. Charitable work, of its very nature, has a positive or negative political meaning. It can be positive, to the extent that it registers a complaint or protest; negative, to the extent that it palliates a situation of oppression that would like to go untouched.

CRITICAL FUNCTION TOWARD THE CHURCH

We are touching here on a delicate subject where it is easy to lose one's way. Because one runs the risk of losing a balanced vision of the religious life, either by maintaining an attitude of supine compliance toward those who command, or by launching forth on fruitless ventures that lead to the breaking down of communion. Between this "rock" of broken communion and this "hard place" of blind compliance lie the conflicts of obedience.

The religious life, as we have repeatedly said, is called upon to proclaim the kingdom of God by constantly bringing to mind the *memoria Jesu et discipulorum,* the remembrance of Jesus' commitment to the kingdom of God, of his healings, of his solidarity with the outcast, of his mercy, and of his uprooted life. Certainly, the whole Church celebrates the *memoria Jesu* in its worship. The Eucharist is no more than the sacramental celebration of this commemoration. But this remembrance must also be proclaimed by the whole Church concretely in its everyday life. And this is where the religious life as a parable comes in— a parable whereby Jesus continues to proclaim the kingdom of God. Christians tend to forget this, and the institutional Church is sometimes tempted, by the very logic of its established character, to forget its reason for being. It is significant that the first monachate came into existence when the Church became established in the empire and, according to Basil and Jerome, the clergy began to adopt a logic of worldly power. The image of the Church of the poor, introduced by St. Francis, certainly did not agree with the feudal attitudes of Honorius or Innocent, the bishops of Rome. Thomas of Celano recounts a significant event: at Damietta, St. Francis of Assisi strove to convince the Christian crusaders not to go into battle, because the violent place their trust in their own arms, and not in God. The crusaders, with their leaders and bishops, laughed at the Poverello, but they suffered a terrible defeat.[1] Mary Ward was condemned to prison because she wanted her sisters, like contemporary male religious, to have a centralized government with a woman in charge. Oddly enough, lay institutes of men and women began to multiply after the Council of Trent, when the Church seemed to be most clericalized.

It goes without saying, of course, that we are speaking of a prophetic service to the Church, for the good of the Church and inspired by a love of the Church. How far a person or group is prepared to go in any concrete case is not a matter of principles, but rather one of spiritual discernment. If, on the one hand, we should avoid an attitude of apprehensiveness toward the governmental structures of the Church, on the other we should not allow religious institutes to be so assimilated as to become the merely passive instruments of the hierarchy, for this would lead to the impoverishment of the whole Church.

CONVERSION TO GOD'S WORLD

History reveals a deep though slow and sometimes retrogressive change in the attitude of religious toward what they have often called "the world." Note that the term "world" can have three different meanings. In the first place it designates the universe which God has created and of which human beings form a part. This is the world that God so loves that he gave his only Son for it (Jn 3:16). Obviously, this "world" has presented no difficulties to religious, and therefore they do not refer to it when they speak of their own proper calling. We should add, moreover, that there have been some religious who have developed a marvelous spirituality of creation. St. Francis of Assisi is perhaps the best-known of these. But St. John of the Cross, he of the "nadas," has nevertheless employed the beauty of creatures in order to speak to us of the Beloved. In the second place, the "world" may designate the distinctive situation of the lay Christian: marriage, family, work, social relationships, culture, politics and economy. In fact, we are dealing here with the world created by God and historically developed by humankind under the influence of a great number of factors. But this "world," precisely insofar as it is a reality fully lived in time by persons leading a normal human life, is counterpoised to the future of God's glory. This is the world to which Paul refers when he says that the married person is concerned with the affairs of this world (1 Cor 7:33). Finally, we have the "world" that is said to be the enemy of Christ, that is, the complex of principles contrary to the Gospel, which tend to dominate social life, such as selfishness, etc. The "world" in this sense does not give rise to theoretical difficulties. In baptism, every Christian renounces it. The problem lies with the "world" in the second sense as a present, secular reality. Ordinarily, Christians live in this reality in a state of tension: fully immersed in it on the one hand, yet at the same time striving to lead it back to God and the glory to come, through faith and hope. The condition of the Christian in this world of history is equally defined by immanence and transcendence. But bear in mind, too, that the Church also forms part of this world, because the Church is nothing more than humanity and history, inasmuch as they are assumed by Christ. Christian religious live this reality in even greater tension, because, on the one hand, they renounce some of the fundamental elements that characterize the existence of secular Christians (family, private property, disposing of their own lives), yet at the same time being unable to exile themselves completely from history.

It was from this human, social "world" that the first monks wished to flee, practicing a total lack of interest in history. For this reason, the early anchorites completely broke off all human relationships. Father Arsenius believed that he had heard the inward command: "If you would be perfect, flee from human beings."[2] This radical flight by the laity, some of whom, according to their biographers, did not see a human face or hear a human voice for years and years, automatically involved a flight from the Church as sacrament and an alienation from the Eucharist. With infinite patience the Spirit of the Lord called them back, little by little, to periodic dialogue, to mutual exhortation and to the Eucharist. Basil, in a letter he wrote shortly after his conversion to Gregory of Nazianz, spoke in pessimistic terms of the situation of Christians living in cities, although he also had to admit that he had brought the evil within himself into the wilderness.[3] Later, when he had been a bishop for some time, he would ask his brothers to come and live near the city, in order to attend to the needs of the sick and of pilgrims. Augustine, on the contrary, created a clerical community to serve the people, but his initiative was unsuccessful, so that monasteries far removed from towns became the common norm. The anonymous author of the *Rule of the Master,* who was the legislator for a number of monks in sixth century Italy, deemed that the world which the monks had abandoned was a situation of sin.

Benedictine monasteries were ordinarily in the nature of walled towns. But they tended to become centers of culture, of agriculture (colonizing the countryside), and part of the economic and political network (the feudal system). Yet the Rule remained clear: both the Master and Benedict insisted that everything, even the garden, be separated from the outside world by a wall, so that the monks enclosed in it might live their lives within it, as in a heaven on earth,[4] to which Benedict adds a further reason: so that they might not hear anything unfitting.[5] It should be noted, moreover, that the prevailing social system favored this sort of isolation, for the feudal lords, too, lived either in country castles or in precincts separated from the rest of the town.

The mendicants broke with this tradition, initially because they lived their religious life amidst the people and were often on the road, and later because they established their convents and small communities in lower-class neighborhoods where they began to exercise daily ministry among the people and where they began to establish Third Order of the laity. Concerning this first stage, although with broader implications, there is a story about the answer some of the first Franciscans gave to Lady Poverty, when she asked them to show her their cloister. "Pointing to the whole world that could be seen from that spot, they told her: 'This, Lady, is our cloister.' "[6]

The new apostolic institutes, starting in the sixteenth century, brought with them a new vision of the human world and of the place of religious in that world. Ignatius of Loyola introduced a principle that profoundly renewed the spirituality of religious when he recommended that his men should seek God, not mainly or exclusively in moments of prayer or in ascetical practices, but "in all things." The Society of Jesus was born "to help souls" through an active apostolate. John of God, Louise de Marillac, John-Baptist de Lasalle, Catherine McAuley and many other founders and foundresses experienced the "world" as a place in which the sons and daughters of God are suffering. They would take their stand over against that world precisely by living a life animated by apostolic charity and mercy, for which reason they would embrace celibacy and poverty, and would enter into community.

Jansenism, together with the widespread distrust of the modern world in the nineteenth century under Gregory XVI and Pius IX, led to a new period of alienation from the world. Under the influence of Jansenism, with its obsessive stress on the rigid demands of a righteous God and on the all-pervasive sense of personal sin, many religious converted their houses into monasteries. Naturally, religious found reasons enough to oppose the worldly environment typified by the life of the court in Paris. Their lives were now centered on expiation and self-sacrifice, whereby they hoped that God might smile on their endeavors. Jansenism left a deep mark on religious communities. Reaction to it began in North America with Isaac Hecker, and gradually gained momentum in Europe with lay movements, until it culminated in the positive and realistic attitude of the Second Vatican Council. Not only the Church, but religious institutes in particular, underwent a conversion to the world created by God and beset by our sins.

In our days, perhaps no one has better exemplified this movement of conversion than Thomas Merton. Converted to Catholicism and the monastic life, Merton rejected both the world and his own rather unexemplary youth. His elitist vision of the monastic vocation led him to assert, in *Seeds of Contemplation* (1949), that secular Christians who wanted to arrive at the experience of God (contemplation) could do so only by fleeing from the city as best they could. "Do not read *their* newspapers unless you are really obliged to keep track of what is going on," was his recommendation. In the December edition of 1949 he managed to attentuate somewhat this pessimistic vision of the world. Later, in *The Inner Experience* (1959), he began to situate the experience of God in the context of everyday existence, and in *New Seeds of Contemplation* (1962) he stated that solitude does not entail separation, and he stressed his positive attitude toward the world. Shortly afterward, as he was praying in his hermitage under the drone of bombers passing overhead, Thomas Merton became a prophet of peace and justice and discovered a new openness toward the religious experience of other religions. He had come back, in a different way, to the world he thought he had abandoned.

Reflecting on this historical experience we must affirm that what distinguishes the religious is a certain kind of presence in the Church and in the rest of the human world. Earlier, we defined it as a critical presence, a challenge. Now we must add that it is always a presence of service. It is for this that religious renounce such fundamental realities as their own family and enter a celibate community where they profess evangelical poverty and join in a common search for the saving will of God. While hermits separate themselves from the world and place themselves in seeming solitude before God, in order to bring the world before him by their intercession, what distinguishes other religious is community. Religious create a distinct structure (celibate community) for different reasons, but always connected with service: the witness of Christian fraternity, the active ministry, or a community of prayer. Members of secular institutes, in contrast, forego community profession in order to sanctify the world under the same societal roof. In our days, there has been a trend among religious to approach the lifestyle of secular institutes, together with a reaction that has stressed a certain kind of monastic spirituality featuring a ''separation from the world.'' Really, separation is a monastic concept. If we apply this to apostolic institutes, it would perhaps be better to speak of ''distinctness,'' whereby they stand as a distinct reality in and before society, by means of the profession of community life. Other items might be discussed, depending on differences of milieu. To what extent religious garb should be different and not merely a reflection of one's dedication to poverty is a matter of mentalities.

THE SERVICE OF GOD

Perhaps we will be better able to understand the various attitudes that religious may take toward the human world if we reflect on the meaning of the way they commit themselves to the service of God.

Divine service has been and is understood in various ways. In systems of static dualism, one commits oneself to the deity by distancing oneself from history and practicing asceticism. The reason for this is that the divine is perceived as something completely diverse and separate, and thus only those who eschew everything but their own salvation and mortify their bodies will be able to encounter God or the divine. It seems clear that the dualism implicit in different ways in various Hellenistic cultures contributed to create the concrete forms whereby the primitive monachate expressed the service of God. These men and women were viewed as ''manservants and maidservants of God,'' not only because they lived in God's presence, but also because they practiced a harsh kind of asceticism. This form of service is missing from the Bible, because the spirituality of the Bible is based on the fact that God created the world and that he is present in history.

A second way of understanding the service of God is in terms of the priestly functions that appear in many religions and, within the Bible, in the tradition of Leviticus. Priests serve God because they offer him worship and care for his house, his rites and his feasts.

A third way of understanding the service of God appears in the Bible, with the prophets. Moses, Ahijah, Elijah and the prophets in general were expressly called "servants of the Lord," perhaps because they were on familiar terms with him (cf. Nm 12:7–8), but more insistently and mainly because (1) God had chosen them (Is 41:8–9, referring to Israel as the instrument of God's will for others; 49:1–5; cf. Jer 1:5), and (2) has anointed them with his Spirit (Is 61:1; Lk 1:15), (3) to save his people (Num 12:7–8), (4) by a message which confronts that people, in their own historical situation, with the truth and love of God (1 Kgs 14:18; 15:29; 2 Kgs 9:36; 10:10; 14:25). In the poems of Deutero-Isaiah, the servant of Yahweh seems to be essentially a prophet, called to lead Israel back to its God (Is 49:5), who suffers, taking upon himself the burden of our sins (Is 53:4–6), and dies for the justification of many (Is 53:10–11). It is significant that the New Testament should have chosen to project the image of the servant upon Jesus in order to explain his mission. Paul, too, calls himself the "servant of Christ Jesus," because he is "called to be an apostle and set apart to proclaim the Gospel of God" (Rom 1:1) and chosen from his mother's womb, like Jeremiah and the servant of Deutero-Isaiah (Gal 1:15). The service of God—Christian *diakonia*—is prophetic in its origins: one serves God by serving his sons and daughters. Even our acts of worship are acts of service to the community.

Here we seem to hear an echo of the prophets: God has no need of our offerings and holocausts; he wants us to be his instruments in the salvation of his people. One indeed serves God by serving his sons and daughters. The most significant achievement of early Christian reflection was its discovery, in the scandal and curse of Jesus' death on the cross, of his unique act of worship. What Jesus did was to submit himself in faith to the mysterious designs of the Father, and by that very fact he saved us from our sins. His unique cultic act was his death, which redeemed the sons and daughters of God. It was in that act that Jesus fully realized his work as the Servant of Yahweh.

We invite those readers who would like to deepen themselves theologically on this theme to reread what Karl Rahner wrote on the unity of the "two commandments" of love.[7] For our intelligence and our love, God is not just one more object among others. He is that mysterious reality, the source of all perceived reality, toward which we tend by transcending ourselves and by transcending every particular object of our understanding or love. Therefore, Rahner concludes, the love of God is not understood when it is interpreted as the object of a particular commandment, as distinct from the other commandments. The love of God is total, and it is implicit in every act of love. It is the basis of all the commandments. One must love God for himself, in his infinite transcendence, and therefore one does not satisfy this vocation to love God by the mere fact of loving any creature. God is always beyond, as the horizon on which all love is set. But from another standpoint, although God touches us infinitely in a way we cannot touch ourselves (he creates us), we cannot reach him directly on this earth. We know him, worship him and love him by way of creation. And we know that it is in the neighbor, generously loved and accepted, that God comes to us as the Other.

The "God alone" of certain contemplative monasteries must therefore be understood correctly. It does not mean that contemplatives pretend to reach God directly (even if they tried to do so through their own inwardness, they would still be doing so by way of a creature!), but, rather, that they seek God always, *without being held back* by any creature. In reality, this is simply the Christian vocation. The dominical sayings on the following of Christ refer to this "God alone," when they speak of the vocation to love God with an undivided heart, with one's whole heart. What the contemplative does is to put himself or herself in the particular conditions of solitude and peace, so that he or she can more fully and freely lift up the world and the Church to God.

IN THE SERVICE OF THE WORLD

This searching for God through his creation, both within and without ourselves, without allowing ourselves to be held back by any creature, is obviously an eminent service we render to the world created by God, because in concrete experience the cares of human beings struggling to carve out their niche in this world tend to enclose them in it. Life in the world is too demanding; it wears us out. From yet another point of view, the very interpretation of the world that has taken shape in the modern age has also tended increasingly to close in upon itself in an immanentistic vision, in which secular values seem to have the last word. Where does this leave eschatology? Human beings are producers. They talk about what they produce or, from a capitalist viewpoint, what they possess. According to some, human beings are complexes of psychic energies, more or less clearly perceived, or else they are the result of liberating or oppressive experiences which psychologists seek to uncover.

The commitment of religious not to be held back by any creature, but to transcend them all in order to stand before God and make their relationship with God the only reason for their life, doubtless presents non-believers with a pressing question: Am I sure that all that I do and live for has full meaning in itself, without looking any further? At the same time, this commitment is perceived as an exhortation by believers: Don't forget that every worldly reality, however wonderful it may be in itself (God created it!), finds its objective fulfillment beyond itself. Paul, or rather the Spirit speaking through him, reminds us: "We know that the whole creation has been groaning in travail together until now; and not only the creation, but we ourselves, who have the first fruits of the Spirit, groan inwardly as we wait for adoption as sons, the redemption of our bodies. For in this hope we were saved" (Rom 8:22–24).

It is upon this fundamental service which the religious life renders the human world that all the other services rendered to society by the various religious families have been built, ranging from the promotion of culture (the monks who copied their codices), to bridge-building in the Middle Ages, to pacifism (Franciscan efforts to bring peace to the embattled walled cities of the late Middle Ages), to the education of youth, care for the sick, burying the dead during epidemics, etc. Despite occasional difficulties of philosophical conditioning, the movement of transcendence followed by religious has frequently led us to a deep love of those who surround us.

Notes

1. *Vita Secunda,* II, c. 4. *Writings and Early Biographies* pp. 388–389.

2. *Apophtegmata Patrum,* Arsenius, 1. *The Sayings of the Desert Fathers* (Kalamazoo: Cistercian Publications, 1973) p. 8.

3. *Ep.* 2. Loeb Classical Library, 190 (Cambridge: Harvard Univ. Press, 1961) p. 8.

4. RM 95, 22–23.
5. RB 66, 7.
6. *Sacrum Commercium*, c. 6. *Writings and Early Biographies*, p. 1593.
7. K. Rahner, "Reflections on the Unity of the Love of Neighbour and the Love of God," in *Theological Investigations* VI (New York: Seabury Press, 1974) pp. 231–249.

Bibliography

J.M. Lozano, *Discipleship: Towards an Understanding of Religious Life* (Chicago: CCRS, 1983) pp. 25–27 (The Kingdom); pp. 72–82 (The World).
———, "Trends in Religious Life Today" in D.E. Fleming, ed. *Religious Life at the Crossroads* (New York: Paulist, 1985) pp. 133–167.
J. Sobrino, *Christology at the Crossroads* (Maryknoll: Orbis, 1978) pp. 41–67.

V ‖ In the Community of Disciples

It should be clear enough from the preceding chapter that the religious life in the broad sense (marked by a commitment to celibacy freely undertaken for the sake of the kingdom) is a life consecrated to the service of God's world. Moreover, we have now and then referred to the particular way in which this type of Christian existence serves the community of believers, the Church. But the subject of the relationships between religious life and the Church is far broader and richer. We are now going to try to understand it.

MOTHER CHURCH

The single theme of Jesus' preaching, and the goal of his ministry, was the divine kingdom that was coming like a grace upon Israel and humankind. That is why every genuinely evangelical faith must go back to this divine kingdom, in order to mesh with the experience from which it sprang. And this is also true of the religious life.

But Jesus did, in fact, gather together a prophetic community of men and women, whom he associated with him in his faith and hope, and in the proclamation and healings which revealed the incipient presence of God's great grace. Jesus was already committed to this proclamation in a celibate life, thus making his own life (more so than that of most of his disciples) into a parable-proclamation of the kingdom of God. For this reason (although, in contrast to John, he was not an ascetic, and in contrast with the votaries of Qumran, he was not a monk), he was taken as a model by all those men and women whose own lives were transformed by grace into so many other parables of the kingdom. When Jesus had been crucified (the prophet of the kingdom of love, excommunicated and blotted out) and the Father had raised him up to the fullness of life, his disciples were drawn into unity by their experience of the resurrection. They were the new community of believers, although they discovered this only little by little. During these early years, Paul, remaining single and gaining his livelihood by manual labor, committed himself to proclaim the in-breaking of the kingdom in the death and resurrection of the Lord. A number of Palestinian prophets also left their homes and occupations, in order to announce the imminent return of Jesus as the Son of Man. Thus there began to appear in the Church, in different forms and with different nuances, what would later come to be called the religious life. Then came the virgins and ascetics and, toward the end of the third century, the anchoritic monachate, followed a few decades later by the cenobitic monachate. Pachomius and Mary, Basil and Macrina, created groups of sisters and brothers. Augustine established first a community of contemplative laymen and later a community of clergy living together with their bishop. It should be noted that this presbyteral community was open to the local church. Basil, after he was ordained a bishop, asked his brothers to open a hospice for pilgrims and the sick on the outskirts of the city.

The religious life with its manifold forms had begun to flourish in the Church. Variety and enrichment of the Church are two distinctive marks that characterize the whole history of the religious life. All those great figures of the past who have set about reflecting on the history of the religious life (we are just now thinking of Fr. Jerome Nadal and St. Anthony Mary Claret) have felt obliged to point out the multiplicity of fruits that this life has produced. Vatican II also does so at the beginning of Chapter VI of the constitution *Lumen Gentium*.[1] And the introduction to the decree *Perfectae Caritatis* highlights the "wonderful variety" of its forms of life and institutions.[2] The decree speaks of the Church as being fecundated by grace, while the constitution speaks of it, in a traditionally feminine image, as the "field of the Lord." The religious life is born of the Church, impregnated by the grace of the Gospel.

THE VARIOUS LEVELS

In fact, the life of commitment to divine service in celibacy is born of the Church on various levels. If the Church is constituted as the eschatological family of Jesus when we hear the word and try to put it into practice (Lk 8:21) or, as Mark puts it, when we fulfill the will of God (Mk 3:35), the Church is also deeply present when a Christian feels called by God to live exclusively for the proclamation of his grace, and commits himself or herself to it. When this happens, the Church is then a grace offered and received, a communion in the Spirit of Jesus, a living faith, an experience of infinite love. This is exactly what we mean when we speak of the Church as the communion of saints. We would insist on this: we think that it is something deeply rooted in the mystery of the Church as a community of disciples that Antony or Macrina, Clare or Francis, Ignatius or Catherine McAuley, Frances Cabrini or Anthony Claret should feel gripped by the Spirit and impelled to serve God in celibacy. Even before anyone around them knows it, they know it. And this reality has been repeated in each of us.

In some cases, the ecclesial reality of the religious life ends here, because not a few Christians keep their commitment to God in the secrecy of their hearts. Many committed men and women had to live and die, unknown and in solitude, during the first centuries of the Church. Today, many Christians live their celibacy amidst the turmoil of the city, without being recognized as such. The fruits of their lives redound to the Church in many ways through their intercession and through the various ministries they undertake as lay Christians. More frequently, however, those who have made the decision to live only for the love of God and of his sons and daughters either create or enter an organization: a religious institute, an apostolic society, a secular institute or some other new type of association. In these cases, the response to grace and the decision to live this way are carried out not only in the mystery of the Church *(in mysterio Ecclesiae)*, but also in its presence *(in facie Ecclesiae)*. This commitment is recognized in varying ways by the community of believers through their leaders, the bishop and the Pope. The life these people profess belongs, then, not only to the inward communion, but to the visible society of the Church, and is subject to certain common and particular juridical norms. It becomes a type of canonically recognized

Christian existence. Grace and response have arisen from the interior depths and come to the surface.

A LIFE FOR THE CHURCH

Since the Church is simply the community of men and women who follow in the footsteps of Jesus, proclaiming the kingdom of God's grace in a world that has no final meaning in itself yet seems to live for itself alone, then every life that is consecrated to revealing the presence of this grace is, in itself, a contribution to the mission of the Church. The religious life is immediately, of itself, a life for the Church.

It accomplishes this service essentially and above all as a life, that is, as a particular type of Christian existence. And this is so, because its essential purpose is to call to mind the kingdom of God, the values to which God himself seems to commit himself throughout our history and, by the same token, the final outcome of that history as promised by God. This is essentially what Vatican II was talking about when it spoke of the religious life as a splendid sign of the kingdom of heaven[3] and as ''a sign which can and should effectively inspire all the members of the Church.''[4] What this means, in effect, is that it is the Church's mission to remind us of the orientation of every Christian life toward God above all things, of the common calling to holiness in the perfection of love, of the Gospel criteria of poverty and of the poor as Christ's representatives, of the value of fraternal communion, etc. That the religious life has done just this, no one can seriously doubt. Of course, there have been many failures. Religious, along with the rest of the Church, have played their part in hindering the laity from coming of age in the Church, and have continued to develop and spread an impoverished theology of the world created by God. But the number and rich depth of the schools of spirituality created by the religious life have surely been an eminent service to the Church.

The Second Vatican Council, in speaking of the religious life as a sign, has viewed it as an evocative presence among the disciples of Jesus. We would go further and say: it is a provocative sign. We spoke above of the prophetic and critical mission of the religious life in the Church. This is something essential to the religious life; otherwise it will fail to fulfill its function of revealing the powerful though incipient presence of the transcendent love of God, because the Church, the whole Church, including religious, tends to accept the values and criteria of the world (the enemy of the Gospel): the logic of power and privilege, of effectiveness and success, of castes and favored classes, of theologies that are not theologies but ideologies defending the status quo. Against all of this, and sometimes despite religious themselves (we are in many ways no better than the rest), the life that religious profess reminds us that such attitudes are contrary to God's logic. The presence of the religious life is always a critical presence. We have already shown in the preceding chapter (and there is no need repeating ourselves here) that the various forms of the religious life and its most representative institutions have always come into existence as a counterpoise to some of the main temptations into which Christians seem to be falling, and as projects aimed at remedying some of the crying needs in the Church and the world.

It is not surprising that the prophetic spirit—through a rereading of history in the light of the Gospel and through mutual exhortation—should occur frequently, although not exclusively, among religious, from Francis of Assisi to Charles de Foucauld, from Teresa of Jesus to the four women martyrs of El Salvador. We said "not exclusively" among religious because, as has often happened, one of the last-mentioned martyrs was a Christian laywoman.

CHARISM AND INSTITUTION

When the charisms of the Spirit who creates the various forms of religious life meet the ecclesial institution which finally accepts and recognizes them, the result is always a fruitful encounter and quite often a painful shock. In order to avoid confusions in the treatment of this two-sided issue, let us first return to the etymological meaning of the words "institution" and "charism." "To institute," in the original Latin sense, means "to set in a determined, fixed place." It connotes a certain public quality: to put something in a place where it can be seen and recognized as such. Secondly, it can mean "to put something in a situation where it can remain solidly protected." The "Church as institution" connotes not only that the grace of God takes on a social aspect among other social entities, but also that the established Church (however ill that expression may ring) is protected by a certain legal order. In being established (as it must) among other realities of this world, the Church gains socially, but tends to lose on a deeper level. Because of this latter tendency, the Church is always in need of the voice of prophecy to remind it of its vocation to transcend the worldly (in the pejorative sense) order of things. A "charism" is a gift granted by the creating and redeeming Spirit of God to various members of the Church, in order to keep the Church on its pneumatic base (*Pneuma:* the Holy Spirit). A charism is an *ecclesial* reality. The Spirit bestows it for the upbuilding of the community of disciples. Therefore, a charism is fully such when the community recognizes it as such. As it rises to the surface of ecclesial life, a charism fecundates the Church. The Church is continually enriched by a multiplicity of charisms, as the entire history of the Church confirms, so that there is no need for us to demonstrate it here.

But a charism, inasmuch as it is a gift of the transcendent yet life-giving Spirit of God, always sows some seed of restlessness in the Church. Because a charism awakens new life and new perspectives, it offers a certain challenge to the ecclesial institution, which is accustomed to the "tried and true." The constitution *Lumen Gentium* gives us an ideal description (and thus a false one, if it is taken as a statement of what always happens), when it tells us that the hierarchy, "in docile response to the promptings of the Holy Spirit . . . accepts rules of religious life which are presented for its approval by outstanding men and women."[5] In reality, these words describe what ought to be and what, in the long run, actually happens. But in sober reality, countless founders and foundresses have suffered exceedingly because of the incomprehension of the community of believers and especially from that of the hierarchy. Despite all the edifying histories that have been written, it is clear that the first anchorites met a great many obstacles on their way to being accepted. In the seventeenth century, Mary Ward was condemned by the Holy Office and put in prison. A papal nuncio judged Teresa of Jesus to be a proud, mad woman because she dared to teach and often left her monastery. Not a few founders and foundresses were removed from the government of their own institutes for a variety of reasons.

The Holy See has recognized all of this in an official document. *Mutuae Relationes* states: "Every authentic charism involves a certain genuine novelty of spiritual life in the Church, as well as a working initiative that may seem inconvenient in its setting, and may even give rise to difficulties, since it is not always easy to discern that it comes from the Spirit.''[6] Exactly: the life that the Spirit brings with his gifts always goes beyond the life which the Church is presently accustomed to. Hence, as the same document states, there is always a relationship between charism and the cross of Christ. No one can be a prophet without dying. One gives life only by being associated in the death of the Lord and, by the same token, in his resurrection. We must accept sufferings as part of the logic of the kingdom of God. Our own founders and foundresses certainly accepted them. Naturally, it is to be hoped that the lessons of the past will also make Church leaders more cautious in these matters. For although it is quite human not to understand the Spirit, and while the appointed task of discerning spirits is by no means easy, there is no great glory in setting oneself in opposition to the Spirit.

INSTITUTIONALIZATION

Every charism eventually becomes institutionalized when the Church-institution recognizes it. But there is a danger in this process. To make religious institutes merely an appendage of the hierarchy—which has been an ever-increasing tendency—would mean emptying the religious life of its prophetic impact. The Second Vatican Council stated that the religious life does not belong, as such, to the hierarchical order of the Church. The religious life is the fruit of a prophetic, charismatic movement which has immensely enriched the community of believers, precisely because it has always offered an alternative to the established order.

Nevertheless, the community has increasingly tried to assimilate the religious life. When the ministerial priesthood came to be regarded as a dignity, most of the monks, and later the Franciscans, ended up being ordained. Then their rules were subject to examination. The Canons Regular, in order to gain exemption from their bishops, put themselves under the protection of the Pope (twelfth century). Then, in order to sidestep the decree of Lateran III forbidding new orders, recourse was again had to the See of Rome. Later, all new constitutions were profoundly revised, and now we have just finished sending even our directories to Rome as well. In the Codes of 1917 and 1983, we are told that the vow of obedience which religious take means above all obedience to the Pope. And this is clear enough, so long as it is understood that we are dealing with an ecclesial institution which is constituted as such by its openness to the whole Church, the universal communion of which is presided over and directed by the bishop of Rome. We can form no Christian community, in the Catholic sense we are proud of, outside of communion with him. But it would be going far beyond the vow in the evangelical and catholic sense reaffirmed by Vatican II to interpret it as something merely disciplinary, demanding passive and blind obedience without dialogue. If this were so, then the religious life would be embarked on a process of institutionalization that would transform religious into mere executors of the hierarchy's will. The religious life would thus lose something that has historically constituted its richness, namely, its critical presence within the Church. Later we will see how evangelical obedience is something far greater and richer than some would like it to be.

THE VARIOUS MINISTRIES

Until now we have been speaking of the fundamental service given the Church by the religious life, precisely in its character as a type of Christian existence. But the religious life has ordinarily been, at least since the twelfth century, the source of different ministerial activities in the service of the community of disciples. Monasticism (the religious life in patristic times) and the Franciscan movement (and, in this, Francis was quite traditional, although he was revolutionary in matters of structure) limited themselves to viewing the religious life as service. The important thing for them was to make the Gospel present in the Church, although the monks eventually accepted various ministerial activities and Francis would decide that their life would have a more complete meaning if they undertook the oral preaching of the Gospel. Even earlier, Basil had come to include the service of pilgrims and the sick in his profession of ''life according to the Gospel,'' and Augustine had opened his presbyteral community to the local church.

Since the twelfth century, with the Orders of Hospitalers, and later with the Trinitarians, Dominicans and Mercedarians, the greater part of religious institutes have been founded for a specific service, that is, for an activity (not just a way of being) that constitutes their ultimate reason for being in the Church. From preaching the Gospel (Dominicans, Vincentians, Redemptorists, Claretians), to Christian education, often of the poor (Brothers of the Christian Schools, etc.), to caring for the sick, the orphaned or the elderly (the Little Sisters of the Poor), to the pastoral care of immigrants (the Scalabrinians, the Sisters of St. Frances Cabrini), to the rehabilitation of prostitutes (the Adoratrices, the Sisters of the Most Holy Redeemer), there is a whole gamut of ministries which is hard to survey in all its breadth. In addition to institutes founded for a particular activity, there are others founded specifically for intercession on behalf of the Church and humanity (the Carmelites of St. Teresa). All of them are what the theoreticians of monasticism would call specialized institutes.

Two important things must be noted concerning these institutes, which constitute the great majority of the orders and congregations in the Church. First of all, their founders and foundresses discovered a particular need in the Church and decided to respond to it with their own personal ministry and with the creation of a new religious family. These many institutes are born, then, to remedy a need sensed as urgent. The Brothers of the Christian Schools, the Christian Brothers of Edmund Rice, the Sisters of Mercy of Catherine McAuley, etc., commit themselves to celibacy in order to be able to devote their lives fully to the care of the poor. The members of the Society of the Divine Word and the Comboni Missionaries become religious in order to give their whole life to evangelization. The first element of their distinctive charism that appeared historically was mission. They often express this in a so-called fourth vow which is, genetically, their first commitment. The Jesuits felt called ''to help souls,'' and added, even before they had decided to become a religious institute, that they felt called to help them wherever the Holy See might judge most urgent and opportune. Teresa of Jesus and John of the Cross ended up founding a different institution, although they had begun with the intention of bringing Carmel back to its primitive contemplative vocation, which Teresa understood as a way of responding to the division among Christians in her day. The kingdom of God, for which one embraces celibacy, seems historically, then, not to have been an abstract ideal, but rather, something quite concrete: the redeeming of the sons and daughters of God. This central and specific element gives meaning to the common elements of the religious life.

In the second place, even these religious must remember that, despite their foundational charism, without which they would be nothing in the Church, they serve the Church above all by their form of evangelical life. They are religious in the measure in which they live in search of God in celibacy, Christian poverty and obedience—and all of these things, in turn, in the measure in which they are expressions of faith, hope and love. Although their life may be oriented toward a ministerial activity, it is the life itself that makes them religious, not their activities (whether prayer or ministry). Religious are such because they live exclusively in the presence of the mystery of God and reveal it by their life, and not because they do this or that more or better. The quality of presence is essential, even should these religious fail to orient this qualifying presence toward one or several activities of service.

It is fitting to remember this at a time when the tendency is to give ministry an ''industrial'' interpretation, evaluating it positively for the quantity of its activities, output and successes. Every Christian ministry is above all a presence, an interpersonal relationship, rather than a mere activity, even when it issues in an activity and is expressed through it. The Little Brothers and Sisters of Jesus remind us of the Franciscan principle of presence; they are making us go back to essentials. The members of institutes founded for a specific end have to make their occupations (intercession or ministerial action) become a mode of presence.

COMMITMENT BEFORE THE CHURCH

The ecclesial reality of the religious life is fully revealed in the public act of commitment. In apostolic societies, secular institutes and other associations, this commitment is in the form of an act of incorporation, with a private promise (that is, not recognized officially as a vow) to live in celibacy, evangelical poverty and obedience. In religious institutes it is in the form of a public vow in the canonical sense. Let us say at once that the canonical difference is clear, although on a deeper theological level it is much less clear. The men and women who publicly commit themselves in this way before their respective institutes had already committed themselves religiously before God when they discovered their vocation and decided to respond to it. Their celibate life of poverty and communion with the saving will of God has its origin in that personal commitment made secretly before God. What they are now doing is renewing it before the Church and committing themselves to it with the Church. Hence, theologically, every act of self-giving, even on the part of members of secular institutes, is, as Karl Rahner saw very well, an act made *coram Ecclesia,* in the presence of the Church. [7]

This act is not just a simple repetition before the Church of the commitment made previously in the secrecy of one's heart. This time the commitment is made public before a group of persons who represent the Church. It is a very human thing to communicate to friends those decisions that deeply affect our lives. We celebrate birthdays, graduations, marriages. But in this case it is not a matter of a merely human act; rather it is a matter of an ecclesial act. The *Rule of the Master* states that monastic promises are made "primo Deo et oratorio isti sancto vel tibi et congregationi": first to God and this holy oratory (i.e., to the saints whose relics are there) and to yourself and the community.[8] The Rule of St. Benedict tells us that these promises are made "coram omnibus" (before all)[9] and "coram Deo et sanctis eius" (before God and his saints.[10] Does this mean that the monastic community is simply the witness of a commitment taken before God? No. The very formulas used show that the commitments were taken before the community and that God was called upon as a witness. In reality, it is a matter of two successive terms: the commitment was made before God through the community. The actual commitment of oneself follows the sacramental structure of Christian religion: God is encountered through the neighbor. The community acts as a visible human sign of the heavenly reality. Both "coram's" ('before's') are to one terminus of commitment. Commitment before God makes one a religious; commitment through the Church reveals the Christian character of the religious life. We commit ourselves to God through his Church. Hence it is that our profession, a public act, pertains not only to the particular community we are entering, but also to the whole Church. Later, in case we fail or undergo a profound personal change, the Church can dispense us from the commitment we made to it, without prejudice to the question of our responsibility before God.

Notes

1. LG, 43.
2. PC, 1.
3. PC, 1.
4. LG, 44.
5. LG, 45.
6. MR, 12.

7. K. Rahner, ''The Layman and the Religious Life,'' in *Theology for Renewal* (New York: Sheed and Ward, 1964) pp. 147–183.

8. RM, 89,6.

9. RB, 58,17.

10. RB, 58,18. .

Bibliography

J.M. Lozano, *Discipleship: Toward an Understanding of Religious Life* (Chicago: CCRS, 1983) pp. 99–112.

F.J. Moloney, *Disciples and Prophets* (New York: Crossroad, 1981) pp. 49–82.

D. Rees *et al., Consider Your Call* (Kalamazoo: Cistercian, 1980) pp. 17–38.

J.M.R. Tillard, *The Mystery of Religious Life* (Saint Louis: Herder, 1978) pp. 1–37.

VI ‖ Calling and Commitment

In attempting to understand the religious life, or more broadly the type of Christian existence created by celibacy voluntarily chosen as a response to the love with which God loves his sons and daughters, we explained it as a type of prophetic existence, a parabolic message in itself, in the service of others. This is its evangelical value and meaning: to proclaim, by the very tenor of one's life, the Gospel of grace. But when we have to pass from the abstract to the concrete and individual, we discover at the very root of all religious life a call and a mission. The religious life commences in God; it is a vocation before it becomes a following.

In reality, this happens in every kind of Christian life and, on an even broader scale, in every human life, because, on the one hand, human beings are much more what they make themselves than what they were born and, on the other, in the case of a human being, the creative word summons up a person who can respond. Hence, the creation of human beings is a creation for grace, for an encounter with God who elevates them above their possibilities in their very existential condition.

Every Christian, like Jesus and in Jesus, feels "sanctified and sent" (Jn 10:36), that is, set apart for a mission. Note well that the Gospel text does not say that Jesus was "sanctified" and then "sent," as two distinct or successive stages, as if the Father chose Jesus for himself and then sent him into the world. In the theology of John, Jesus belongs to the Father radically, from the very beginning. "He chooses him and sends him" really means "He chose him to send him," or simply "He sent him.'' The same can be said of every Christian. Every Christian belongs totally to God, his or her Creator, has been redeemed by the blood of Christ and consecrated with the seal of the Spirit in baptism. The only thing remaining for the Christian to do is to discern in faith which concrete existential situation God is moving them toward as the milieu in which they must encounter God, growing toward him in love and serving him in his sons and daughters. What all Christians are trying to do is to discern their proper mission on earth, and not whether God wants the more or less for himself. God chooses us all for himself and for his people. And he calls us all to the fullness of love (of God and neighbor). The Christian is called to discern the concrete situation in which he or she will best be able to tend toward this love and radiate it.

On this profound level, it cannot be said that God ''sets apart and sends'' some Christians (for example, those whom he calls to the priesthood or the religious life or a secular institute), while he leaves the rest aside. This would be setting out from a pagan concept of God, in which only some things (related to worship) belong to him. Marriage and so-called secular activities proceed from God; they belong to him.

We ask the reader's pardon for hammering away at this so insistently. On the one hand, we are trying to open a breach in the walls of a theology that has been giving us an interpretation of the religious life for centuries. On the other hand, it seems that we are sometimes being offered a new elitist interpretation of the religious life and the life of secular institutes that goes beyond (or, rather, falls behind) the teachings of Vatican II. As late as 1977, Hans Urs von Balthasar began speaking of ''states of election,'' and has stated that the ''calling to the state of election is a qualitative, special, differentiated calling. There is no similar calling to the secular state, which is characterized by the lack of such a calling.''[1] This is not a matter of being a somewhat different state; it is a matter of being qualitatively the only state of election. All of this is based, as can be seen in the pages that follow, on a mistakenly literal interpretation of the Gospel sayings on the following of Christ, which literally demand material renunciations. We find something similar in the absolute value that some would like to attach to the idea of ''consecration.'' We will treat of this, too, toward the end of this chapter. It is significant, also, that the expression ''state of perfection,'' which the council sedulously avoided in dealing with the religious life, has made a fleeting appearance in a pontifical document.[2]

MINISTERIAL VOCATION

But if every Christian is set apart and sent, each individual receives a personal mission. And among these missions there are some for which God chooses certain persons to be the spokespersons and signs of his grace before all people. God calls persons to particular ministries in the community. This is well known by those lay Christians who, in increasing numbers, feel called to perform evangelizing and helping activities beyond the limits of their own families. Every ministry is an offer of grace made by God through a human being. Every ministry presupposes, then, a particular kind of participation in the mission of Christ, the one Mediator. The Christian community needs ministers, and the Spirit sends them to us.

It is in this sense that we must understand the distinctiveness of the calling to the religious life. Since the Church needs married couples, mothers and fathers, lay ministers to work in the upbuilding of the Church through various services, along with ordained ministers entrusted with the gathering together of the community (bishops, priests and deacons), the Lord Jesus calls various Christians to these various vocations in the Church. The Lord also calls a minority of Christians to actualize, by the very tenor of their lives, the remembrance of Jesus and of his message concerning the kingdom of God. This is where the distinctiveness of the religious life lies: not in any supposed fact that they belong to God more than others, but in the fact that, while God chooses lay Christians to animate by faith, and direct toward the kingdom, those various types of existence that are founded on the created order of things, he calls religious to express, by the very tenor of their life, the message of the infinite love of God that is not exhausted in creation. It is clear that celibacy for the sake of the kingdom speaks both of the transcendence of grace and of its presence among us.

And, nevertheless, the people of God were not mistaken in calling even the first anchorites and cenobites "servants of God," because the religious life is in itself, independently of any personal perfection, a public revelation of the service of God in the world, to which we are all called. The religious makes "religiousness" not only the soul of his or her life (all Christians must do this), but the only motive and reason for the type of existence he or she embraces. The religious life acts, so to speak, as a mirror held up to our common relationship with God.

VOCATION AND CHARISM

Having clarified the distinctiveness of the vocation-mission of religious among other Christian vocations, we must now try to understand what is really meant by a vocation. We have said that the process through which a vocation is discovered is a gradual discernment of the future that God has in store for us in faith. This means that we do not have total certainty, yet we still have certainty enough to decide to follow this vocation. When this certainty is reached, the Christian feels that God is questioning or calling him or her to something. What the Christian hears is the creative and redeeming word of God, that is to say, not a word that just says something, but one that effects it—except that God waits for our response, in order to effect it. It is he who is going to make us secular or religious, lay or ordained Christians. This word is discovered in the depths of our being, as a grace and an energy. Following our vocation is nothing more than allowing this grace to be actualized in and through our lives.

Paul saw a close relationship between Israel's vocation and its charisms or graces (Rom 11:29). Paul himself explained the various situations of Christians, not only by having recourse to the notion of calling or election (Rom 1:1; 1 Cor 1:1; 7:20), but also to that of charism. A charism or a creative gift of the Spirit is, for Paul, the basis for marriage, for celibacy (1 Cor 7:7), for being an apostle, a prophet, a minister to the poor, or community presider (1 Cor 12:5–11, 28–30; Rom 12:5–8; cf. Eph 4:11–13). Again, following one's vocation means opening oneself to those gifts of the Lord that make it possible.

This presupposes, in everyone who is called, an attitude of faith. The various Christian vocations have their source in God and constitute a particular experience of God in the world. They are carried out as Christian vocations in the measure that they are undertaken in faith, facing and accepting the mysterious designs of God's love for oneself and for the rest of his people. What really makes a type of life to be Christian is the fact that the one who follows it effectively encounters God in it, in faith, hope and love. When this happens, that life becomes diaphanous, radiating the presence of the divine mystery. It is the vocation of a Christian.

But the fact that every Christian life begins with a vocation and is founded on certain charisms presupposes, moreover, a periodical rereading of our lives in faith, because the vocation to a type of Christian life in the service of the Church is only a part, although an important part, of our vocation as persons. Only the future will gradually disclose to us our mission. And the experiences that we go on acquiring in time will also go on modifying us deeply. No one knows what it really means to be married or single, a father or mother, or a religious, until concrete experience has revealed it to them. Our theology of the religious life will also change over the years. And we will have to return periodically to put ourselves in God's presence in order to receive anew his creative word. Times of crisis are times for listening in faith.

COMMITMENT AS RESPONSE

Once the Christian has perceived with sufficient certainty the kind of Christian life and service to which he or she feels called, it becomes a matter of his or her responsibility. The paradigmatic Gospel accounts of the calling of the first disciples of Jesus, which are meant as models of the Christian vocation, culminate in the call of Christ: "Follow me." But this call is immediately followed by the disciples' response: "They left all things and followed him." We are aware that we are making the same type of application of the Gospel text as many other religious, who have felt strengthened in their own religious calling by meditating on it. The Gospel account speaks to us, in fact, of the call to conversion and faith, and not of a vocation to a determined kind of life. But there is no doubt that the structure of the experience is the same in both cases. From yet another standpoint, it is in that kind of life that the disciple is going to live his or her relationship with Christ in the concrete.

Generosity in obeying ("they left all things") is for everyone. This means that all Christians are called to choose the way in which they may better encounter God themselves and help their neighbors to encounter him when they make their vocational decision. The precept of loving God with all one's heart is for everyone. Here again, we run into the persistent theological prejudice which regards the layperson as a halfway Christian, whenever it is stated that religious give themselves totally to God and when their commitment is described as a holocaust. Laypersons, too, are called upon to give themselves totally to the love of God when they follow their vocation. And as we already said above, this fullness of love is not opposed either to conjugal love or to earthly possessions. The love of God runs at a far deeper level and animates everything else.

A married Christian layman feels called by God to incarnate his experience of God's love in a relationship with another human person and to constitute with her and their possible children a community of disciples. The Christian who, out of a variety of circumstances, realizes that his or her destiny is to remain single discovers that a certain type of solitude is an integral part of his or her path toward Christian maturity. Something similar happens in the case of a widow or a widower, but here their solitude is peopled by a remembered presence. Those who feel called by God and the Gospel to celibacy know that they are called to a universal kind of love which in itself more clearly reflects the transcendence and universality of Christian love. All of these Christians—married, single, widowed or celibate—give themselves, consecrate themselves to a grace that comes out to meet them along their different paths.

The various kinds of Christian life begin when the individual disciple of Christ commits himself or herself to one or another type of existence. The matrimonial commitment is of its very nature a public one, since it is made with another person and thereby tends to impact the very constitution of society. However, the decision of a layperson to remain single as one's own special path toward God, or that of an individual who embraces celibacy for the sake of the kingdom, can, of itself, remain within the confines of one's own relationship with God. The decision to embrace celibacy, even before that decision becomes publicly known, and even if it is never formalized in a public commitment, already creates a type of religious life, the meaning of which comes from a relationship with the transcendent love of God. In this deep sense, all those who make such a commitment are already religious, that is, they make relationship with God to be the only wellspring of their life. In this sense we may say that there are not a few religious who are not religious in the canonical sense. Pius XII, in two discourses delivered only a few months apart in 1957 and 1958, dwelt on this theme. In the first discourse he recalled the fact that there are a number of Christians who commit themselves to celibacy out of love for God and neighbor, through a commitment known to God alone.[3] Some of these Christians, he added in the second discourse, do so in order to follow privately a contemplative vocation.[4] Naturally, in the measure that these Christians wish to belong to a movement recognized by the Church, their commitment must be recognized by the Church. It must in some way be made *in facie Ecclesiae,* in the presence of the Church. This is the process that leads to the rise, not only of the religious life in the canonical sense (by way of public vows), but also of apostolic societies, organized in community after the manner of religious institutes, and of secular institutes, which are distinguished from the former by not including a commitment to community life. In these cases, we have three forms of life which are publicly recognized by the Church and which are, hence, canonical.

THE EXPERIENCE OF GOD IN THE
COMMITMENT OF A RELIGIOUS

When we set about reflecting on the wide and varied gamut of commitments that create a kind of Christian life, we are struck by the fact that among all of those we have just mentioned, in contraposition to those of laypersons who marry or decide to remain single, there is a common element. All of them embrace celibacy for the sake of the kingdom of God. There are laypersons who embrace celibacy in order to lead a life exclusively dedicated to prayer or in order to consecrate their life to certain active ministries. The members of secular institutes, apostolic societies and religious institutes do so, in their distinctive ways, as part of an organized movement. But their fundamental option is the same.

What is the typifying element in the religious experience that is common to all these groups, namely, an experience marked by celibacy? Celibacy for the sake of the kingdom implies, as we shall later see, that in those Christians who follow it, the experience of the love of God is translated into the adoption of this love and of the bond which it creates as the only reason explaining their type of life. The motto *Deus solus*— God alone—is not the exclusive property of contemplatives. What it means is that every decisive interpersonal relationship is set aside, and that one's life is built exclusively around one's relationship with God. It is a global experience, because it takes over one's whole life, and a unifying experience, because one develops one's whole life around it. At the same time it is an experience of the love of God as infinite and transcendent. God transcends all things (which are his creation) and comes forth to meet his sons and daughters, in order to lead them toward himself in ultimate love. The commitment of a religious (on the deep, pre-canonical level mentioned above) is a response to this divine love in its transcendent and universal dimension. This is the very thrust of the renunciation of matrimony and property.

Obviously, this commitment has meaning only within the context of faith, because only one who has a lively faith in the love of God and in the promise of his kingdom could make the sacrifices entailed. Certainly, faith is the root of every Christian life as such. It is faith that radically opens up a person and a life to the mysterious presence of God beyond all things and in all things. But a secular life can have full meaning without faith, although it would then cease to be a Christian life. One can be married or single without faith; one can be a politician or an economist without being a believer. But one cannot be a religious without faith, because the vision of faith is what induces religious to give themselves to God and to build their whole life around their relationship with God alone (in the Christian sense of the word). A religious life that is lived with weak faith and faint-hearted love ceases to appear religious, even though one leading such a life remains materially faithful to the vows.

Both the world and the Church expect religious above all to radiate this faith in the love of God, both in their persons and in their life. Neither the world nor the Church expects first and foremost that religious should set apart more times for prayer or perform more activities. Rather, they expect them to be men and women of lively faith who remind others that above all human loves, sorrows and sufferings, the love of God stands firm. And it is precisely this commitment in faith to God's love that will make them into Christians of prayer and effective ministers of the Gospel. The need for a life visibly built around Christian faith and love is more pressing than ever today, given the growing secularization of society. In the Christianity of former times, faith could be expressed publicly in many ways. Today it has become something of an underground river. In large cities, who knows whether one's neighbors are believers or what religion they belong to? On our various "sabbath days" many of us go off to our different churches, temples or synagogues, but just as many or more either stay at home or go for an outing to the country or the beach. Often, even Christians belonging to the same church recognize one another only when they gather for worship. In the rest of their life, secular values rule, without reference to the Creator.

ELEMENTS OF THE RELIGIOUS LIFE

The history of both theological reflection and of canonical norms on the essential elements of the religious life is somewhat surprising in this matter, because it took theologians and canonists a little more than six centuries to arrive at the three fundamental commitments which today are undertaken, in their distinctive ways, by religious and members of secular institutes. In describing (not defining) the monastic life, the Fathers and the first anchorites offer us a number of characteristic traits. Real poverty is rarely lacking. Mention is also made of incessant prayer, of solitude and of being pilgrims in this world. Other remarks relate to ascetical practices: fasting, abstinence, vigils and the like. Bishops, often living among a married clergy, call attention to the fact that monks are celibate *(agamoi)* and that nuns are virgins *(parthenoi)*.

However, when it comes to the realities to be renounced by those who profess the monastic life, the various masters seem to have a sharper focus. Family and possessions are the main things to be renounced in the *Precepts* of Pachomius and in the *Asketikon* of St. Basil (fourth century).[5] Evagrius of Pontus speaks of living alone, and of abandoning country, family and riches.[6] Cassian tells us that they must renounce riches, family and all visible things.[7] It should be noted, in order to understand what these men are saying about renouncing one's family, that in the classical world marrying did not mean creating a new family, but continuing one's own, by introducing one's wife into it. Celibacy, therefore, meant going out of one's own family, leaving it behind. Hence, when these early monastic writers deal with the renunciations made by monks, they speak mainly of celibacy and poverty, occasionally adding some third or fourth object. The same tendency is seen in the Fathers. In their biblical commentaries, John Chrysostom and Ambrose join celibacy and poverty as two similar realities.[8] Augustine speaks of celibacy, poverty and entering community as the distinctive traits of the monastic vocation.[9] It should be noted that, even when they are searching for a third element to form a classic triad, they do not choose obedience. We have found only a single text, in the works of John Climacus (seventh century), which refers to the renunciation of goods (poverty), family (celibacy) and one's own will (obedience).[10]

If we focus on the commitments that the members of fraternities and monasteries began to make, we note that St. Basil alone, among all their leaders, imposed on adolescent candidates a virginal consecration similar to that made by women. He lamented that while women were being consecrated virgins, thus committing themselves to that type of life, men were making no such public commitment, and that therefore the bishop could not chastise them for their failure to observe it. Sulpicius Severus expected aspirants to make a promise of obedience (to the rule).[11] Aspirants made this commitment upon being accepted when the rule was explained to them for the first time. It was the anonymous Master (ca. 500 A.D.) who first introduced the making of a promise of obedience in the oratory at the end of Prime.[12] St. Benedict (ca. 560 A.D.) asked for a triple commitment of stability, conversion and obedience.[13] Note that both these rules demanded a prior formal renunciation of goods as a necessary prerequisite for aspirants. These were to be the three promises made by monks and nuns in the West. In the twelfth century (more precisely in 1148), there appeared in the abbey of the canons regular of St. Genevieve in Paris the commitment to chastity, communion and obedience.[14] By "communion" was meant, obviously, the sharing of goods in common. The new formula of commitment, which came to take its place alongside monastic commitment, developed within the canonical movement as one of the results of the reform of the clergy, because it was obvious that monks were celibate by their very vocation, whereas the clergy could only be expected to practice celibacy by having it legally imposed on them. And it was by no means obvious, despite the efforts of numerous reformers, that the clergy could not dispose of private property. The vow of obedience was regarded, more for social and juridical than for disciplinary reasons, as essential for the formation of community. Thus it was said that one gave himself and his things to a particular church or monastery, understood in the context of the feudal system.

A half-century later, the beginning of the Trinitarian rule, approved by Innocent III in 1198, states that "the brethren must live under obedience to the prelate of the house, who will be called the minister, in chastity and without property."[15] The same Innocent III, in a letter written in 1202 to the abbot and monastery of Subiaco, after referring to the obedience that is due to the abbot, goes on to state that "the renouncing of property and the keeping of chastity are so united to the monastic rule, that not even the supreme Pontiff can dispense with them."[16] On several occasions Innocent had to combat the possession of private property by the monks of certain monasteries. The letter to Subiaco condemns this.[17]

One asks oneself whether this was not the result of a change in the social system at a time when private property became the basis of society. The change from a vow of "communion" to one of being "without property" might reflect this change. It should be observed that the Trinitarian rule does not expressly mention anyone's having to make a vow concerning the three elements referred to, and that Innocent's letter to Subiaco refers not to vows, but to essential traits of the monastic life. But what is important here is that these three elements are already considered to be essential. This new triad, in the same terms as were used in the Trinitarian rule, appear in the rules of the Friars Minor. In our opinion, this did not come from an initiative on the part of St. Francis of Assisi, who could not have known of this recent development, but rather from suggestions of the Roman Curia, who usually drew their inspiration from previous documents. From the Friars Minor, the expression passed into the rule of the Poor Clares, which was approved by Innocent IV in 1253.[18] It was that Pope who declared that chastity, the renunciation of property, and obedience were essential to the religious life. Shortly afterward, Thomas Aquinas popularized this doctrine in his *Contra Impugnantes Dei cultum* (1256), *De Perfectione vitae spiritualis* (1269), *Contra pestiferam doctrinam retrahentium homines a religione* (1270), and finally in the *Summa Theologica* (1270).

GENESIS AND VARIETY OF COMMITMENTS

Recently, scholars have begun to question the value that should be attached to this triple commitment, which has generally come to be regarded as the norm in the religious life since the end of the twelfth century. There is an important distinction to bear in mind here. It is one thing to question whether or not religious must explicitly make these commitments (for example, Basil's *Asketikon,* Augustine's *Praeceptum* and Benedict's *Regula Monasteriorum* do not provide for them); it is another to question whether or not these three elements form an essential part of the religious life as a form of life created by the Holy Spirit in the Church, quite aside from the question of whether Church law prescribes them or not.

The charism or gift of the Spirit that creates this type of Christian life is without doubt what impels and enables a Christian to embrace celibacy for the sake of the kingdom, because by a religious we mean pre-

cisely a person whose whole life is built exclusively around relationship
with God. Here, then, we have the root of every kind of religious life,
understood in its essential, theological sense. We would add that more
frequently, although not necessarily, this relationship with God around
which the celibate tends to develop his or her life is determined by a
specific vocation, either of intercession (contemplative) or of active service. Many Christians embrace celibacy in order to be able to consecrate
themselves more readily to prayer or to some ministerial activity. At any
rate, whatever the specific orientation their life might take, there are celibates for the sake of the kingdom who feel called to live their vocations
fully in secular life. These persons may prefer to remain isolated, not
seeking any official recognition by the Church, or else they may choose
to be enrolled in some movement or association (secular institute or a
more flexible kind of association) and thus receive recognition from the
Christian community, both directly for their belonging to an organization
of Christian life and indirectly for their commitment to celibacy. In all
of these cases, celibacy is accompanied by some sort of vocation to solitude.

There are other Christians who feel called by God to live in some
degree of counterposition to secular society. Among these, some feel
called to live a contemplative life in solitude, far from the prevailing network of human relations. Theirs is an eremitical vocation. In these cases,
the vocational gift for solitude acts to complete and radicalize their option for celibacy. In fact, the first anchorites (etymologically, "anchorite" means "one who is withdrawn") understood their solitude as a
radical kind of celibacy whereby they tended to live a life cut off from
social relationships. This is why their counterposition was understood as
a "flight from the world." In contrast, many more Christians feel called
to a community founded not on mere natural sociability or on the relationship between the sexes, but on the Gospel. A communitarian charism
tends to complement the charism for celibacy by giving celibates for the
sake of the kingdom an immediate place in which to grow and experience
their love for the kingdom. The community is the fundamental structure
through which these Christians express their counterposition to civil society, of which they form part in varying degrees. Monks have tended
to interpret this counterposition through the old expression, received
from the anchorites, of a "flight from the world." In fact, monks living
in community soon invented the structure of cloister, and Vatican II

stated that it is proper of the monachate to serve God within the walls of the monastery, even in those cases where they have undertaken certain apostolic activities.[19] It is clear that, even in more recent interpretations of monastic life, community always functions as a fundamental note. In this, however, they differ considerably from apostolic communities, which are oriented toward mission. Apostolic communities have tended to live their counterposition to the world as a "critical presence," which is at once an active service of and a challenge to society, with both attitudes being inspired by their love for God's world.

We can summarize what we have said thus far on the variety of Christian celibate commitments in the following diagram:

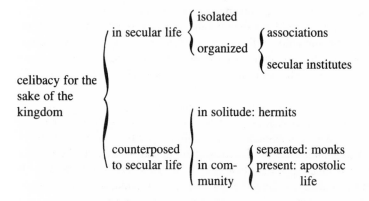

Going back now to examine the elements that create the various forms of life consecrated through celibacy (with the exception of the diocesan or secular priesthood in the Latin rite) and comparing these elements with the traditional commitments of the religious life, we discover the following data. In the first place, among the three promises required in the Rule of St. Benedict, we find that one of them—conversion of life—included celibacy, although it was probably more all-embracing, since the conversion envisioned was not understood in a purely moral sense, but as an orientation of one's whole existence to God alone. The other two promises relate to community life. Since monastic community life is essentially a relationship of obeisance to the magisterium of the leader, there was a promise of obedience. Then, partly in reaction to the crisis which the monachate was undergoing in St. Benedict's time, but also for deeper reasons, the Rule added the promise of stability. Among the canons regular of the Augustinian tradition, we find a vow of celibacy (chastity) and two vows of community: communion (of goods) and obedience. But we know that among both the monks and the Augustinian brotherhoods, the cession of private property was a requisite to being accepted into the community. The vow of communion only affirmed it explicitly.

When the vow of communion of goods was changed to that of poverty (Trinitarians, 1198; Franciscans, 1215), members took a commitment to poverty in the sense that all private property, both individual and communitarian, was excluded. This was a distinctive feature of the Franciscan movement: a special vow. Later, the commitment to poverty has been understood as a renunciation of all private property and as a sharing of goods, and in this sense the vow again became an element of community life. On the manner in which the vow of poverty has been understood, we will have to be more precise when we come to study this matter expressly. In the formulation which has since become common, we find ourselves with the fundamental commitment to celibacy, plus two communitarian commitments. Clearly, the members of secular institutes must interpret this matter differently, since they do not profess community life. Moreover, when the present Code (1983) requires that hermits also make these commitments, poverty is interpreted as a simplicity of life as close as possible to real poverty, and obedience (to the bishop) is interpreted as a bond of communion (not with one's own community, since none exists) but with the local church.

SELF-GIFT: A CONSECRATION?

We mentioned above that we are currently running the risk of attributing an absolute, and in some way exclusive, value to the consecration proper of religious and secular institutes, when we speak of "consecration" or when we say that "consecration" is the basis of the religious life.

Turning briefly to history, we note that the term "consecration" is alien both to primitive and medieval monasticism, with a few isolated exceptions (for example the consecration of young men as virgins in St. Basil). The fact is that the vocabulary of "consecration" belongs to the cultic language of the priesthood, whereas monasticism appeared as a lay movement. Scholasticism did not stress it. For St. Thomas, what founds the religious life is the act of self-giving, made in profession. Hence, he speaks constantly of obliging oneself *(se obligat),* promising *(promittit),* entrusting oneself or one's own life *(deputat, exhibet),* giving oneself *(praebet),* to give oneself as a servant *(mancipare).* He uses the verbs "to consecrate" or "to be consecrated" in a very incidental way. In *Contra Impugnantes,* he says that "perfect religion is consecrated to God by a threefold vow."[20] In his *Commentary on the IV Books of Sentences,* under the influence of Pseudo-Dionysius, he understands the action of the priest who receives a profession, as a "consecration" in a very broad sense, namely, as a petition for graces whereby the religious professing might be able to remain faithful.[21] Finally, in the *Secunda Secundae,* Aquinas is obliged to have recourse to the concept of cultic consecration in the strict sense, in order to explain why not even the Pope can dispense from a solemn vow, his reason being that whatever has been consecrated to God cannot be made profane.[22] This argument is objectionable on a number of counts. To begin with, it has recourse to a taboo and to a concept common to many pagan religions. Moreover, it applies the static consecration of a material object to the consecration of a human person, without taking into account the values and problematic of human freedom. In brief, the term "consecration" has very rarely been used throughout history in order to describe the religious life, and those rare uses have been unhappy ones.

In the Second Vatican Council, precisely in the more traditional and monastic treatment given the religious life in *Lumen Gentium,* the verb "consecrate" and the noun "consecration" are used to explain the meaning of the act of self-giving and obligation to service which, in Thomist theory, constitutes the foundational act of the religious life. In this connection, the council reminds us that baptism is the fundamental consecration of every Christian, but that religious, "in order to derive more abundant fruit from this baptismal grace, make profession of the evangelical counsels in the Church . . . in order to be free from hindrances . . . and in order to be more intimately consecrated to the service of God."[23] *Perfectae Caritatis* uses the more specifically Christian concept of the "following of Christ" as the fundamental reality of the religious life. But in number 5, while describing the religious profession of the evangelical counsels in terms of God's call as its originating act and to the religious' self-gift as the human response to that call, the decree returns to the explanatory notion of consecration, nuancing what had been said previously in the constitution: ''This constitutes a special consecration, which is deeply rooted in their baptismal consecration and is a fuller expression of it.''[24]

What is the source of so much insistence, after the council, on consecration as the basis of the religious life, and of so many attempts to deduce everything from this one concept? Perhaps it would be better to speak of several sources. There are certainly those who would like to impose an elitist and reactionary vision of the religious life. They would like to set religious apart, as beings ''above'' the confusion of this world, and at the same time to remind them that their true greatness lies in the renunciations they have made, albeit out of the love of God. Back to the search for individual perfection, to separation from the world, to passive obedience of execution. Nothing could be more suitable for this, of course, than to remind the religious that he or she is a ''consecrated person.'' But aside from this unworthy interpretation, there is the quite different case of the influence of the new Code of Canon Law. We already mentioned in our introduction that Pius XII, in an attempt to discover a new term that would cover all institutes, whether religious or secular, hit upon the expression ''states of perfection.'' But Vatican II, in dealing expressly with the theme of the religious life, declined the use of this concept. This, as we said, left us without a common name, so that one had to be sought for the new Code. The expression *Instituta sequelae Christi* might have been chosen, not only as being a key concept in the New Testament, but also as being clearly better-rooted in tradition. Instead, the Code chose to speak of ''Institutes of Consecrated Life'' in the title of the section dealing with them, and of ''life consecrated by the profession of the evangelical counsels'' in the opening line of the text of the first canon.[25] The regrettable thing here is that later, in the course of the other canons, the clarifying note ''by the profession of the evangelical counsels'' seems to be dropped, thus appearing to give religious consecration an absolute and exclusive value, which was certainly not the intention either of the drafters of the Code or of the Pope, since no one could have intended to deny the value of the consecration of baptism and of confirmation, let alone that of the particular consecrations that are based on it (priestly consecration, for example). But there is a great danger of forgetting all this when one sets about constructing a theology of the religious life with a starting point in the notion of consecration.

LIFE CONSECRATED BY CELIBACY

St. Thomas was right in saying that the foundational act of the religious life is the act whereby a person commits himself or herself to the service of God, understood—we would add—as a way of living predicated exclusively on relationship with God. We should round out St. Thomas by saying that the primary foundational act is the grace of vocation, of charism, to which the human person responds by a commitment (the foundational act on the part of the human being). This cannot be clearly understood as an act of "consecration" in the strict and proper sense, because such a consecration is always effected by the ministers of the Church. But in the case we are dealing with—as both Cajetan and Suárez ably noted—the important thing is what the person who is professing does, and not the prayers whereby the minister solicits the grace of God. From yet another viewpoint, the one who receives the profession is not properly the priest, but the religious community—often a lay community—represented by its superior. A profession made without a priest being present is perfectly valid.

A solution to this problem may be found in an attentive reading of the words most commonly used by St. Thomas, and of the council texts based on them. It is religious themselves who commit their persons and their lives to the service of God. In this broad sense one may speak of consecration. This is not, we repeat, a consecration in the strict sense, which in the Church, in the case of persons, is always effected through a sacrament: baptism, confirmation, matrimony, ordination. The fundamental consecration is that of baptism. Nothing is deeper, more intimate or more total than this. *Lumen Gentium* states that in profession, religious are "consecrated more intimately to the service of God."[25] More intimately does not mean more deeply (than baptism)![26] Rather, it means carrying the baptismal consecration to a more intimately lived experience. It is an existential dedication. In fact, *Perfectae Caritatis* modified the expression of *Lumen Gentium* by stating that "this special consecration [of religious] . . . is deeply rooted in their baptismal consecration and is a fuller expression of it."[27] Exactly: the person is already totally consecrated in baptism. What the religious life does is to express before all people, by a life dedicated to religious values, this common consecration. For this reason, it is not proper to speak of the religious life as "consecrated life" without further ado, but as a life consecrated through celibacy or, as the Scholastics used to say, "through the evangelical counsels."

Notes

1. *Christlicher Stand* (Einsiedeln: Johannes Verlag, 1977).
2. *Redemptionis donum,* 4.
3. AAS, 50 (1958) 36.
4. AAS, 50 (1958) 566–567.
5. *Praecepta,* 49: PL, 23,73. *Reg. fus.,* 8: PG, 31,936.
6. *Tract. ad Eulogium,* 2: PG 79,1096.
7. *Conlat.,* 3,6: SC 42, pp. 145–146.
8. J. Chysostom. *In Primam ad Corinthios,* 9,2: PG 61, 77. Ambrosius, *De Viduis,* 11,71–12,74,: PL 16, 255–257.
9. *Enarrat. in Ps.* 103, 16: PL 37, 1371. CSEL, 40, 1513–1514.
10. PG 88,657.
11. *Int.* 7: PL 103,498. *Ep.* 199,18: PG 32,720B.
12. RM 89, 8–16: SC 106, pp. 372–375.
13. RB 58, 17–20.
14. Odo, abbas S. Genoveffae, *Ep.* 1: PL 196, 1399.
15. PL 214,445.
16. PL 124, 1066.
17. Cf. PL 124, 709.
18. Innocentius IV, in J.H. Sbaralea, *Bullarium Franciscanum,* 2, p. 474.
19. PC 9.
20. 1.1, c. 1.
21. *In Sent.* IV, dist. 2, q 1 a 2 ad 9.
22. 2-2 q 88.
23. LG 44.
24. PC 5.
25. CIC, can. 573, 1.
26. LG 44.
27. PC 5.

Bibliography

E.F. O'Doherty, *Vocation, Formation, Consecration and Vows* (New York: Alba House, 1971) pp. 13–24.

M.B. Pennington, *Called: New Thinking on Religious Vocation* (New York: Seabury, 1983).

K. Rahner, *The Religious Life Today* (New York: Seabury, 1976) pp. 23–27.

D. Rees *et. al., Consider Your Call* (Kalmazoo: Cistercian, 1980) pp. 13–24.

J. Sikora, *Calling: A Reappraisal of Religious Life* (New York: Herder, 1968) pp. 9–28.

Universal Call to Holiness and Religious Vocations. Donum Dei 11 (Ottawa: Canadian Religious Conference, 1966) pp. 15–44.

A. Van Kaam, *The Vowed Life* (Denville: Dimension Books, 1968) pp. 75–112.

VII ‖ Celibacy for the Sake of the Kingdom

Throughout the whole preceding part of our study, we have had to touch repeatedly on the theme of celibacy. The reader will by now have grasped the reason why. Celibacy voluntarily embraced for the sake of the kingdom of God is the originating charism of the religious life; it is the gift which orients one's whole existence in one of the most essential areas of human personality, namely, that of interpersonal relationships and sexuality. We have not—by far—said all that needs to be said about this matter. In this chapter, we would like to dwell for a while on the meaning and value of religious celibacy.

THE TERM ITSELF

While the term obedience has always been used to designate what would later be the object of a vow, and while the term poverty has been changed only two or three times throughout history, celibacy seems not to have received a satisfactory designation until the present. Initially, the term used was *virginity,* but although this would aid in the development of a spirituality of spousal relationship with Christ, the term itself referred to a condition of feminine anatomy, thereby giving it not only a future orientation, but burdening it with various legacies from the past. Virginal consecration was explained in a Greco-Roman context in which a virgin was sacred by the mere fact of being a virgin. In fact, one Pope ordered that those virgins who had been violated by barbarians should be kept separate, in order to hide their shame, from other monasteries of virgins. Likewise, Tertullian declared that all virgins were sacred, even those who were thinking of getting married later.[1] On occasion, the term virgin was also applied to men, although they were more commonly referred to as "continent" and the virtue they practiced was commonly referred to as "continency."

Later, *castitas,* chastity, became the preferred term. Here again, however—at least in the Greco-Roman mind—a chaste person was one who abstained from sexual relationships, although in an isolated instance St. Augustine spoke of the chastity proper to matrimony. The reason for this is clear: from a Christian point of view, chastity consists in submitting the sexual instinct to the Gospel, in any state of life, whether single, married or widowed. The term chastity cannot, therefore, be used restrictively to designate the commitment of a religious as such. The expression perfect chastity was also used in this context, but it, too, is not adequate, since it seems to imply that married chastity is not perfect. It should be borne in mind that the perfection of a virtue does not derive from the degree of abstinence it imposes, but from the intensity of love with which it is lived and practiced. The chastity of a celibate can be less perfect than that of a married person.

For these reasons, St. Thomas said that what religious really commit themselves to is perfect continence, that is, to total sexual abstinence.[2] But this, too, had the drawback of centering the question on just one aspect, namely that of physical abstinence, which is also central in Manichaeism and Gnosticism, although it is not accorded that much value in the New Testament. Despite the observations of St. Thomas, the term that came to be preferred after him has been *chastity.*

We cannot help asking why St. Thomas spoke precisely of *perfect or total continence,* or why the term later preferred was *chastity,* since, if we analyze the commitment made by religious and the members of secular institutes, the reality which first comes to mind is celibacy, with its renunciation of the matrimonial relationship. The first thing that these kinds of Christians commit themselves to is not the cultivation of a virtue (chastity is likewise cultivated in Christian matrimony), but a kind of life. Even the commitments to poverty (formerly, communion of goods) and obedience refer, above all, to a style of life.

The explanation is to be found in the traditional view of matrimony, expressed by St. Thomas, as being essentially ordained toward procreation and the alleviation of the sexual instinct. Lacking from this way of viewing matrimony is the very modern view of matrimony as an interpersonal relationship aimed at the mutual development of the spouses—a point of view adopted by Vatican II in *Gaudium et Spes*.[3] In the narrower view, which was very common, the commitment to sexual abstinence or chastity, understood in the same narrow sense, was thought to be sufficient to express the renunciation of the reality of matrimony. Today, with our fuller vision of matrimony, this is not so. People who commit themselves to the religious life today mainly renounce the interpersonal relationship of love in marriage, and not just its physical aspects. For this reason, the *Normae secundum quas,* given in 1901 for institutes of simple vows, defined the object of the vow as a commitment to observe celibacy and also, by a new title (in virtue of the vow), to abstain from every act contrary to chastity.[4] The Code of 1983 tells us that the evangelical counsel of chastity "entails the obligation of perfect continence in celibacy."[5] The 1901 *Norms* seem to us to be better formulated, since they speak directly of celibacy and of the kind of chastity that is proper to it. Thus we prefer to use the more biblical expression, "celibacy voluntarily embraced for the sake of the kingdom of God." This brings out more explicitly the overall human value of the commitment in question, and not merely or mainly its physical aspect.

CELIBACY AS AN EVANGELICAL VALUE

While Israel valued the virginity of a woman as a preparation for marriage, the Scriptures of Israel presented marriage as a universal calling and sex as a gift of God. Thus, throughout the history of the chosen people there was no precedent that would lead anyone to embrace chastity for religious motives. The religious thing to do was to marry. Jeremiah alone tells us that God forbade him to marry, because he wanted to use his solitude and childlessness as a warning sign to Israel: it had no future (Jer 16:1–4). The Genesis call to matrimonial union and procreation (Gn 1:28, 9:7) dominates Israel's entire spirituality. In Judaism this is a matter taken quite seriously. There are some very strong rabbinical sayings against men who do not want to get married. These men, according to a traditional saying, are the first among the seven classes of men excommunicated by heaven (= God) itself.[6] A man was obliged to marry very early, and this was especially true of the disciples of the rabbis. Nevertheless, it seems to be in Jewish Hellenistic milieus, around the first century, that the age for contracting marriage began to be postponed somewhat.

Therefore, the following renunciation-saying, attributed to Jesus solely by Matthew, would have shocked or even scandalized many: "For there are eunuchs who have been so from birth, and there are eunuchs who have been made eunuchs by men, and there are eunuchs who have made themselves eunuchs for the sake of the kingdom of heaven. He who is able to receive this, let him receive it" (Mt 19:12). Jesus was talking of a voluntary renunciation of conjugal love, for religious reasons, not imposed by nature or by other human beings. This was profoundly new. Some years ago, J. Blinzer already called attention to the fact that Jesus would not have used the term "eunuch," which was a serious insult in Israel, in a laudatory sense, except as a response to a malicious insinuation, because to be a eunuch was not merely to have a condition that was offensive to male pride, but, rather, one that had religious connotations. Castrated animals were considered unclean, and men who had similar defects were not allowed to participate actively in worship (Lv 22:24). In Jesus' time, traditional Jews sometimes used the word "eunuch" as a reproach to those young men who dressed in the Greek style, which was deemed effeminate. If Jesus used this term, it was because some adversary had used it in a polemic attack. Thus we would have a confirmation of the tradition that Jesus personally embraced celibacy. Jesus would be saying that he, and possibly others after him, were renouncing conjugal relationships for the sake of the kingdom of God.[7]

It is not hard to grasp what this *logion* is trying to say. The incipient in-breaking of the kingdom of God, the culmination of all history, in which Jesus believed and which he proclaimed, was urgent enough to except some persons from the common law of Genesis. The latter lost its binding character in the face of the arrival of that greater grace which is the kingdom. Jesus had decided to live exclusively in the expectation of the definitive grace, in order to proclaim it and in order to reveal its presence in his healings of the sick. The celibacy he embraced had a prophetic character: it was tied to his proclamation and was at the same time a symbolic reality, a dramatized parable whereby he confronted others with the transcendent importance of the kingdom.

CELIBACY IN PAUL

The second text of the Christian Scriptures (this time a whole section) which speaks to us of celibacy is chapter 7 of the first letter of Paul to the Christians at Corinth. Paul deals with it in response to the first of a series of questions that these Christians have addressed to him. The way in which the saint answers them leads us to suppose that the Corinthians, under the influence of the spiritualistic anthropology of Hellenism, were beginning to lay exaggerated stress on the fittingness of "not touching a woman." Paul answers them by harking back to the anthropology of Genesis: the normal course is that "each man should have his own wife and each woman her own husband" (1 Cor 7:1–2). Nevertheless, the words that follow make it clear that we are not only under Genesis; it is well for the celibate and widowed to remain as they are (1 Cor 7:8–9), even despite the saying of Genesis 2:18 that it is not good for man to be alone.

In Paul's view, there is, underlying both matrimony and celibacy (considered as two types of life in faith), a divine charism (1 Cor 7:7). This is a very important point. This charism is a permanent vocational gift, one which Paul regards as a way of contributing to the upbuilding of the Church. He speaks in his own name and person, basing what he says on his own experience, because in this matter he has "no command of the Lord" Jesus (7:27). It seems rather strange that Paul was celibate, especially if it is true that he had been a Pharisee equaled by few in his observance. Had his wife died? Or was she, perhaps, also a member of a Pharisee family and refused to follow her husband along the new way, thus forming an occasion for the so-called Pauline privilege (1 Cor 7:15–16)? These are mere hypotheses. What is certain is that, whereas the relatives of the Lord and Peter himself traveled in company with a Christian woman, Paul had renounced this (1 Cor 9:5). Why this preference? The apostle gives two reasons. The first of them is eschatological: the final crisis with its tribulations is imminent, the time is quickly drawing near. Paul does not ask couples to separate, but only asks that those who are not bound in marriage should not seek to be married. Paul here reflects the mistaken conviction of the primitive Church which wanted to translate the eschatological situation into a calendar. He believed that the end was near and that it did not, therefore, make much sense to get married. Some think that this undermines the value of what Paul has to say about celibacy. But in reality we know that the eschatological meaning of Christian existence, after the cross and resurrection of the Lord, is something independent of chronology. We are in the definitive situation of humanity, and this means that the Genesis call to matrimony and procreation is not the last word. Secondly, Paul also offers another Christological and ecclesiological motive for celibacy, which is intrinsically valid in itself.

He explains the Christological and ecclesiological meaning of celibacy further along in this passage, when he sets up an antithetical parallelism between the celibate person and the married person, first in masculine, then in feminine terms: "I want you to be free from anxieties. The unmarried man is anxious about the affairs of the Lord, how to please the Lord; but the married man is anxious about worldly affairs, how to please his wife, and his interests are divided. And the unmarried woman or girl is anxious about the affairs of the Lord, how to be holy in body and spirit; but the married woman is anxious about worldly affairs, how to please her husband" (1 Cor 7:32–34). It is clear that the apostle is speaking about two types of Christian existence, not of marriage and the single state in general. "Is anxious" indicates the occupation characteristic of each of these states. The term *areskein* (to please) has a strong sense in Paul. It indicates a strong orientation of love. Both kinds of life are described from two points of view, namely that of occupation and that of a love relationship. The celibate, says Paul, is occupied with the affairs of the Lord, that is, with the interests of the risen Lord. Basing this on what we know of Paul's own experience, we might translate the "affairs of the Lord" in terms of the churches, the preaching of the Gospel, etc. And the celibate lives this concern with an orientation toward the love of the Lord.

More problematic in this passage is its description of marriage, bearing in mind that it refers to married Christians, as compared with the description of the celibate Christian. Paul tells us that it is proper for a married person to be concerned with the world (in the good sense of the world created by God: *the* world, not *this world*) and to live in a relationship of love with one's spouse. Of course we do not have a total theology of Christian marriage here. For do not married Christians also receive those charisms whereby the Church is built up? Paul picks out in Christian marriage those traits that characterize it as a marriage, and not those which characterize it specifically as Christian. He himself presupposes that the married person lives for the love of the Lord and his affairs, and that for this very reason, as Paul sees it, the married person lives in tension. Perhaps this will be better seen if we add to the description of celibate existence the word "only": the unmarried man or woman is anxious only about the affairs of the Lord, how to please him.

It should be noted that, for Paul, celibacy and matrimony are two positive realities and that they are fulfilled through a relationship of love: exclusively with the Lord in the case of the celibate, with one's spouse (and both with the Lord) in the case of the married. Both kinds of life also suppose a concern, an occupation: creation (increase, multiply, possess) in matrimony; the Church, preaching, various ministries in celibacy. One is not celibate, then, in this sense, simply because one does not marry. Moreover, Paul does not expressly mention physical relationships. For him, both matrimony and celibacy presuppose an overall interpersonal relationship.

AN ORIENTATED LIFE

The saying attributed to Jesus in Mt 19:12 speaks of "eunuchs who have made themselves eunuchs for the sake of the kingdom of heaven." This saying refers to a decision ("have made themselves"), but, above all, to a type of existence. In the case of Jesus himself, this type of existence was totally oriented toward the expectation, proclamation and manifestation of the kingdom, that is, of God himself in his mysterious plan of salvation, because the kingdom or reign is essentially God himself imposing his love upon our evils. In contrast, Paul speaks to us of celibacy as an existence that develops around a relationship of faith and love with the risen Lord, and through working on behalf of his Church. Note that what both texts are saying boils down to basically the same thing, because the reality that Jesus expressed under the symbol of the kingdom (the liberating grace of God) burst into history with his own death and resurrection. This is already a Christian interpretation, but it points to the same thing. And the Church is born around this experience. Now we can say either that we become celibate for the kingdom of God, or that our celibacy consists in living for the love of the Lord or of God in Christ, and in being occupied with his affairs.

In both cases we have an existence which is shaped around the experience of God's love for us (the kingdom), and which is oriented toward proclaiming and radiating it. What radically constitutes celibacy is this relationship of love toward God and the neighbor, embraced as the only reason for one's being, to the exclusion of any other interpersonal love relationship, even one that might be a determinant in another type of life, such as marriage. What counts above all is to love and spread love, not above all to abstain from a certain type of love. Without this determinant relationship of love, one may well be a bachelor or a spinster, but not a celibate in the theological sense spoken of by Jesus and his apostle Paul. Note, too, that we are speaking of a profoundly human love, because to say that a particular form of love is charity simply means that it is a participation in the love of God, a gift received from him; it does not mean that it is not deeply human. This love is revealed in presence, in self-giving, in compassion and in affectivity.

We would like to insist on the fact that this orientation of love, which we call celibacy, refers at once to the Lord and his affairs, that is to say, it is a global, overall love which embraces both God and the neighbor or, if you will, God and all those sons and daughters of his that he wants to save. Celibacy, virginally undertaken in a pure relationship of love with Christ, as the patristic writings on virginity bear witness, came at last to exercise an ecclesial function. The virgin represented the Church. Later, men and women religious would embrace celibacy in order to commit themselves more fully to an external ministry or to one of intercession for the Church. Celibacy, like the love that inspires it, is very concrete. One embraces celibacy, for example, in order to be able to dedicate one's whole life to the service of the poor.

A UNIVERSAL, PREFERENTIAL LOVE

If we compare conjugal love with celibate love, we will at once note an essential difference between them. Conjugal love entails a deep commitment with another person, and this commitment affects other dimensions of both parties, including their deep religious attitudes. Celibate love, a total giving of oneself in love, presents itself above all as a universal love, excluding any determinant commitment with another human person. In this case, the individual's commitment is with God, the source of all love and the wellspring of all goodness. We should add that, when we call this love "universal," we do not mean to imply that it is simply left hanging in the air or in the abstract. Quite the contrary:

the person who lives this universal love is ready and willing to live this relation of religious love with every person who crosses his or her horizon.

From this first characteristic, a second characteristic derives. In conjugal love, the two parties are established in a unity of the same nature ("two in one flesh," as the Bible puts it) and thereby enter into a communion in intimate areas from which others are excluded. In celibate love, even when it is incarnated in lively friendship with one or more determined persons, there is no zone of communion which may not be created with others. Even though celibate persons give themselves in friendship, their self-gift does not include that exclusive right which spouses give to one another. By that very fact, too, the element of physical bonding proper of married love is lacking in celibate love.

This gives rise to a third characteristic of celibate love: it presupposes some kind of solitude. The persons whom the celibate loves come and go. Often, too, they are separated by distance. The celibate often finds himself or herself alone, in an aloneness which must be peopled by the love of God, the never-failing companion.

Nevertheless, even within this universal scope, the Christian celibate's love must be preferentially oriented toward certain persons: the needy, the suffering, those who lack love. One embraces the universal love of celibacy precisely in order to be able to project God's love and ours upon those who have the greatest need of love. Jesus proclaimed the kingdom for everyone, yet he healed the sick, mixed with the outcast multitude and sat down at table with tax collectors. We must repeat, then, that celibacy, not only in the ministries it creates, but also as the kind of love it is, is preferentially orientated toward the "poor," the marginated, and those who are suffering, whether physically, morally or spiritually. This explains why in this case, too, Christian love becomes "political" when it is present and active among marginate or oppressed groups or masses.

CELIBACY AND OTHER CHARISMS

We have already seen that, for Paul, the option for marriage or celibacy is explained by different gifts that God grants to different Christians. In these cases, the gifts are not of the sort granted for some

transitory activity (e.g., speaking in tongues). Rather, they are permanent, vocational gifts, not directly aimed at performing activity, but at
leading a type of existence. The diversity of gifts is understood by Paul
in reference to the one Church which the many gifts contribute to up-
build. Celibacy is not given mainly or solely for one's own perfection,
but rather to enrich the community. In reality, this fundamental charism
of the religious life receives a more highly specified content from other
vocational charisms. There are two other charisms which give rise to two
different types of celibate life within the religious life. The first is the
gift which prepares some persons for the eremitical life, that is, a life
lived in solitude, apart from human society. Here, celibacy gives rise to
a type of Christian existence where the sociability of the human being is
developed on an interior level, as prayer. This is undoubtedly a radical
form of celibacy. But even in this type of celibacy, if it is lived fully,
dedication to the Lord's affairs cannot be absent. This dedication is carried out in the intercession whereby the hermit brings before God the
sufferings and joys of the world. The Christian contemplative lives his
or her belonging to the world from within God. We have already referred
to the examples of Teresa of Jesus, Thérèse of Lisieux and Thomas Merton. But this concern for the Lord's affairs may also lead the hermit to
incursions into society. Antony went to Alexandria to debate with the
Arians, when he learned that they were alleging that he was of their number.[8] And Merton made his presence felt in society through his letters
and books.

Ordinarily, however, religious celibacy is fulfilled in a vocation to
a form of common life, founded exclusively on the quest for the kingdom
of God. This is the community charism. In this case, the universal love
proper of celibacy finds immediate expression in relationship with one's
brothers or sisters who share this common life. The community, a network of interpersonal relationships born of the Spirit, then becomes the
sustaining force of the celibacy of its members. Entering a community
entails that one feel called to friendship, that is, to a type of a love that
seeks the good of others.

The community one enters may be a community founded for an active, external ministry. The charisms which equip one for these various
ministries then offers the celibate members of these communities certain
channels through which they can express and nourish their love. This is
apostolic celibacy, such as Jesus lived and, after him, Paul.

CELIBACY AND FRIENDSHIP

In the preceding paragraphs, the theme of celibate friendship has arisen more than once. The question has become more pressing in our days, given the liberty which men and women religious enjoy in our open society. In the past, especially since the sixteenth century, there was a great deal of talk about "particular friendships" between members of the same community. The warning to avoid them was sometimes based on the fact that such friendships could harm the communion which one professed toward all the members of the community. Another reason given was the unhealthy character of an intense, affective relationship with a person of the same sex. Sometimes this particular friendship was felt to be a potential source of political conspiracy during community elections, especially among small, enclosed groups. In still other instances, it was perceived as a descent of the person to a level on which physical attraction was preponderant. It was seen as a lack of love for the rest, or a factor devaluing celibate love. In one way or another, this type of relationship was fostered by the excessively closed character of the environment. In our times, we tend to think of closed environments in terms of the classic instances of jails and concentration camps.

Today the problem of friendship takes on a broader character. It is obvious that celibacy does not entail the renunciation of friendship, even of friendship with persons of the sex one feels attracted to. In the past, this was a much more difficult matter, owing to certain social conditionings. Religious institutions were isolated and isolating. Despite this, when certain relationships developed among celibate persons, say, with one's spiritual director, intense friendships could occasionally develop. We do not know exactly to what point Francis of Assisi resonated in the presence of Clare, or Clare in the presence of Francis. Nevertheless, the sources suggest that the relationship that existed between them was at once very spiritual and humanly felt. In the case of Francis de Sales and Jeanne de Chantal, their letters speak clearly enough for themselves. The friendship between them was both tender and respectful. Obviously, the type of relationship in such cases varies considerably according to the varying social surroundings. But there is one thing that does not change. Between celibates, there can be friendship on the level of affectivity, mutual esteem and support, without the existence of attraction on a physical level, although even this may come with the passing of time. This friendship, to the extent that it allows the expression of pent-up affectivity, may even be a help to celibacy and afford the celibate some measure of psychic balance. On occasions, this friendship is marked by an intensely spiritual character. Men and women, already liberated by the love of God, may experience a relationship in which the Lord is explicitly present as the expressed bridge or point of reference. Such a spiritual relationship can be invested with a kind of affective tenderness, without thereby engaging the mechanisms of sexual attraction.

From the way in which we have understood celibacy, as an orientation of love with a universal character, it may be deduced that celibate love requires, above all, a deep respect for the fundamental commitment made by the celibate. Not only is it necessary that there be an absence of exclusive commitment and of sexual intimacy with one's friend; for celibacy itself begins to lose its spiritual force when the other person begins to weigh so heavily in the affections of the celibate as to become a limitation on his or her liberty. In that case, celibate friendship would be heading in the direction of the essentially distinct affective form of conjugal love.

DIFFICULTIES

Celibacy entails difficulties all its own, as a way of life. We do not intend to dwell on those difficulties that arise from the fact that celibacy may be undertaken under the impulse of a false vocation in which sexually linked psychological factors have played a determining role (fear of the opposite sex, sometimes quite clearly fostered by a mother who has failed in her marriage; the experience of a broken home, etc.). The fact that one is not called to marriage does not mean that one is automatically called to celibacy. But it should also be noted that no one is so sanguine as to hope that those called to celibacy will be free of all conditioning. Full liberty of this sort simply does not exist. But one's vocation does exist, when the religious motive is active and has a strong influence on one's decision. During the course of one's life, the adverse conditionings which accompany one may cease to exist.

The first difficulty that someone living in celibacy may experience is the progressive drying up of his or her affectivity, so that celibacy ceases to be an experience of love. Love is always concrete, always the love of this particular person. When love is not based on the unique character of this particular person (as happens in conjugal love), but, rather, relates to this or that person mainly for what he or she has in common with all others (their being children of God, for example), it can run the risk of not reaching the person in his or her unique personal reality, and therefore may become, instead, a mere abstraction. The lack of truly interpersonal relationships fails to nourish and sustain love. The celibate must make a constant effort to encounter each person in his or her concrete reality. The celibate also needs to find some outlet for his or her affectivity. For this reason, the celibate's main support is prayer, in which the believer experiences the love of God and learns from God how to love his creatures.

From yet another standpoint, there is the danger of not learning how to fully accept our own sexuality. The celibate who is truly such, that is to say, the person who is animated by a lively love for the Lord and the neighbor, is keenly aware of his or her own sexuality. This consists precisely in an ability to relate to oneself and others with a loving attitude. One is then very much aware not only of the value of the person, but also of that person's being a man or a woman. It is only when true celibates realize the cause of the love that moves them that they will be capable of fully accepting their own sexuality and orienting it as they ought. It is much easier, and far more harmful, not to undertake this responsibility, preferring instead to devote one's life to protecting oneself, thus rendering oneself incapable of developing a free and at the same time delicate friendship with another. This is often the result of a deficient education, or it may be the consequence of unresolved problems, but it can frequently indicate a lack of authentic Christian love. It is easier to defend oneself from love and be destroyed for the lack of it than it is to enjoy the freedom of love that Christ offers us. It is much easier to be a bachelor than it is to be a celibate for the sake of the kingdom of God.

But it is also much more painful. It is not hard to find, in communities or parishes, men and women who are materially celibate, yet who appear to be consumed by resentment, sometimes low-keyed and passive, but sometimes openly aggressive. Lacking in enthusiasm and quick to criticize, they are distrustful of every initiative that might give life. In its depths, even their prayer life seems to harbor a certain resentment toward God. They are individuals who have not been capable of developing their affectivity or of finding a system of sound relationships as the motive and sustenance of their loneliness.[9]

Notes

1. R. Metz, *La consécration des vierges dans l'église romaine* (Paris, 1954) p. 51.

2. 2-2 q 186 a 4.

3. GS, 48–49.

4. *Normae,* n. 129.

5. CJC, can. 599.

6. Pes. 113b.

7. J. Blinzer, "Eisin eunochoi. Zur Auslegung von Matth. 19,12," ZNTW 48 (1957) 254–270.

8. VA 69. *The Life of Anthony,* p. 82.

9. Cf. Marin W. Pable, OFM Cap., "Psychology and Asceticism of Celibacy," in M.A. Huddleston, I.H.M., *Celibate Loving* (Ramsey: Paulist Press, 1984), p. 23.

Bibliography

L. Boff, *God's Witnesses in the Heart of the World* (Chicago, CCRS, 1981) pp. 116–132.

T.E. Clarke, *New Pentecost or New Passion?* (Paramus: Paulist, 1973) pp. 95–107

Consecrated Celibacy. Donum Dei 16 (Ottawa: Canadian Religious Conference, 1971).

D.L. Gelpi, *Discerning the Spirit: Foundations and Futures of Religious Life* (New York: Sheed and Ward, 1970).

M.A. Huddleston, ed., *Celibate Loving* (New York: Paulist, 1984).

C. Kiesling, *Celibacy, Prayer and Friendship* (New York: Alba House, 1978).

D.M. Knight, *Cloud by Day, Fire by Night* (Denville: Dimension Books, n.d.) I. pp. 59–113.

J.B. Metz, *Followers of Christ* (New York: Paulist, 1978) pp. 60–62.

E.F. O'Doherty, *Vocation, Formation, Consecration and Vows* (New York: Alba House, 1971) pp. 117–172.

M. Oraison, *The Celibate Condition and Sex* (New York: Sheed and Ward, 1967).

J. Ridick, *Treasures in Earthen Vessels: The Vows* (New York: Alba House, 1984) pp. 29–83.

A. Van Kaam, *The Vowed Life* (Denville: Dimension Books, 1968) pp. 292–298.

VIII || The Poor, Citizens of the Divine Kingdom

For some seven hundred years, now, religious have been explicitly making a vow of poverty. Recently, secular institutes have been making the same commitment. The reason is, that from St. Thomas Aquinas on, poverty has been numbered among the three "evangelical counsels" which, in the somewhat individualistic view of Scholasticism, constitute the liberating means that facilitate the attainment of perfection in charity. It should be noted here that the Fathers, who coined the term *counsel* as part of their defense of marriage, pointing out that celibacy was not obligatory, occasionally linked poverty to virginity as basic character-istics of a type of Christian life to which one makes a free commitment in response to a vocation. One may even say that in the writings of prim-itive monasticism, poverty appears with singular forcefulness, even more explicitly than celibacy, while obedience is notable by its absence.

But the term *poverty* covers a number of different realities in the various types of religious life, and even includes various elements within each type. We are now going to examine the meaning of the term within the various kinds of life devoted exclusively to proclaiming the kingdom, as they have appeared throughout history.

POVERTY IN VARIOUS FORMS

While the virgins of the Church in imperial times did not consider poverty to be part of their vocation, it found early acceptance in Christian asceticism. Origen, whose viewpoints paved the way for the birth of monasticism, stressed not only sexual abstinence, but also the privation of material goods, as distinctive traits of the life of the perfect. He himself embraced both, and the monachate at once followed suit, making a public and total renunciation of property the initial act in a monk's career and the official manifestation of the commitment he made before God. We could say that it was the equivalent of a profession. The monk had to effectively divest himself of all his goods and distribute the proceeds among the needy, thus becoming as poor as they were. Monks would reject every candidate for formation who had not effectively left everything behind, thus committing himself to God's providence.

This initial act, later called *disappropriatio* (self-divestment), came to be the permanent point of departure for all forms of religious life. It should be noted that, initially, this act of divestment was essentially linked to solidarity with the poor. The influence of Mt 19:21, the text most commonly cited in this context, was decisive. Later (in Egyptian monasteries, in the *Rule of the Master* and in the Rule of St. Benedict), candidates were allowed either to distribute their goods among the poor or to cede them definitively to the community. Thus, the connection with the poor was no longer considered essential. In canonical legislation it was eventually lost. The important thing was to divest oneself of one's goods.

In the primitive, anchoretic monachate, what counted essentially was to embrace the painful condition of the poor. Poverty was spoken of as lack, as insecurity, and therefore as a source of suffering. But this, too, would disappear in cenobitic monasticism because, on entering a community which was often corporately rich in goods, one embraced a comfortable level of life and acquired a new security. The rationale here was that the important thing was not personal poverty, but the communion or sharing of goods, for which one was prepared by renouncing the private possession of these goods.

Starting with this initial renunciation, the various forms of poverty began to be differentiated.

For the solitary, poverty meant a most austere life, sustaining oneself by one's own work, the complete avoidance of saving or hoarding, and distributing any remainder among the needy. For the cenobite, it meant dependency, caring for the goods held in common and working, often intensely, during the entire time prescribed for work. Later (thirteenth century), St. Francis of Assisi returned to the ideal of real poverty, with the renunciation of individual as well as collective property. Poverty meant becoming as poor as the poor and with the poor: working as the simple folk worked, or begging for food, undertaking an itinerant life like that of the many beggars of the time. The Franciscan ideal was adopted by St. Dominic and later by the other mendicant orders. The vow of communion or sharing was changed to that of living "sine proprio," without property.

The mendicant experience came to exert a profound influence on the way poverty would be understood from then on. Religious kept on making the vow of poverty, although it was understood in most cases as individual self-divestment and the sharing of goods. From then on, poverty demanded some sort of simple and austere lifestyle, and simplicity in buildings and furnishings. At least this was the theory, because, in practice, religious often built great palatial buildings for their living quarters. Currently, in Europe and Latin America, many of these buildings now serve as libraries, barracks or seats of government. Poverty became primarily an ascetical means of perfection through dependence, and it could be quite demaning on the individual level.

The Institutes of Clerks Regular included in their commitment to poverty the renunciation of ecclesiastical benefices, as well as that of not accepting dignities in the Church without the express permission of their major superior or a mandate from the Pope. The reason was that ecclesiastical "benefices" (a parish, a chaplaincy, a seat on the cathedral chapter) were supported by real properties, often great ones, bequeathed and endowed by the faithful.

Apostolic institutes adopted several other aspects of poverty. Not a few of them were founded expressly or at least preferentially for the poor: schools, orphanages, old-age asylums or hospitals. It should be borne in mind that all institutes for the care of the sick or the elderly founded in the seventeenth through nineteenth centuries were for the poor. Only the poor were taken into hospitals and hospices, since the latter offered no services which the rich could not equally or better obtain in their own homes. Not a few of the institutes of Christian education were founded expressly for the education of the poor.

In our own day, solidarity with the poor—either political (defending their rights) or effective (giving public witness by adopting as closely as possible the situation of the poor)—has begun to give a new orientation to poverty in all these institutes. In apostolic institutes, this has often led groups to leave institutions of service (which, in the United States and Canada, were founded for those who were once poor but no longer are), in order to create new services for the new poor.

THE POOR IN ISRAEL

Confronted with this evolution and great variety of concepts of poverty, it will be helpful if we turn to the Bible, in order to discover the place of the poor in scriptural revelation.

In the Scriptures of Israel, the poor are spoken of as those who are in a material situation characterized by privation and suffering. Since God has paternally provided the earth and its fruits for the sustenance of all (Gn 1:27–30, 9:1–7), poverty has always been viewed by Israel as an evil contrary to the will of God. Wisdom literature, in its advice to the young man in search of wisdom, generally speaks of poverty as the possible outcome of his sin, laziness, dissoluteness or lack of foresight. In contrast, the prophets view the poverty of many Israelites as the result of the sins of the powerful.

As for riches, they were traditionally viewed by Semitic peoples as a sign of divine favor. God multiplies the children and cattle of the just man: Abraham, Solomon and Job, for example. Nevertheless, it did not escape the attention of traditional wisdom that riches have often been the cause of various sins: pride (Prv 23:11), lack of faith (Prv 30:9), and, above all, of no longer putting one's trust in God (Ps 52:9; Prv 11:28). On the other hand, even though the proud pauper is ridiculed on one occasion (Sir 25:2), poverty is not viewed in the Bible as a source of sin.

This faith in creation which we alluded to above, the belief that everything is a gift from God and must be received gratefully and responsibly, made it practically impossible for Israel to regard poverty as a religious value, and much less as an ascetical one, in the way that the Greeks would later do. But with poverty as a starting point, a very intense spirituality developed in Israel. In various psalms, the poor express their faith in God and state that God is their treasure and their refuge. The poor, the *anawim,* while acknowledging on the one hand their misery, proclaim the greatness and the love of God on the other (cf. Ps 9:10–14; 10:12–14, 17–18; 1 Sm 2:1–10; Jer 17:7, 14, 17). Zephaniah invites the humble of the earth to seek justice and humility, in order to find refuge on the day of the Lord (Zeph 2:3). The idea of the humbled who seek

God tended to give rise to the idea of the "remnant of Israel" (Zeph 3:12–13). Note that the humble are always set against the background of a real situation of suffering or privation. Out of this situation, virtues are born. Poverty here is a spiritual attitude of one who is suffering from poverty.

THE GOSPEL AND THE POOR

In the ministry of Jesus, poverty returns to its original sense of a situation of suffering that is contrary to the love of God, independently of the inner attitude of those who suffer it. The poor are associated with the blind, the leprous, the deaf-mute and the dead, in the response Jesus gave to the disciples of John the Baptist (Mt 11:5), and with prisoners, the blind and the oppressed, in Jesus' sermon in the synagogue of Nazareth (Lk 4:18–19). Jesus sees his healings as a sign that the kingdom of God's compassionate love is already dawning (Mt 12:28; Lk 11:20). For this reason the poor, too, receive the good news of their liberation, because when God finally establishes his reign, there will be no more poverty or suffering. This is the meaning of the threefold beatitude, preserved in its original sense in Lk 6:20–21. The poor who suffer from hunger and are weeping are happy, because all of this is going to end.

At the same time, Jesus confronts riches as a humanly insuperable difficulty for entering the kingdom of God, because riches enslave the heart and prevent that attitude of faith, hope and generosity that Jesus preaches. In an almost paradigmatic scene, Jesus deals with a rich man who wants to be his disciple, by telling the latter of the need to orient his life totally to the kingdom of God by renouncing all things. We have already said above what this really meant: not necessarily to abandon these goods materially or by a legal act, but, rather, to rise above them and entrust oneself to the reign of God. We believe, as we have already said, that this passage (Mt 19:16–29), the story of the call of a disciple, did not originally mean that Jesus (despite what is said in Mt 19:21) was requiring material abandonment, but rather that the rich man should turn totally to God and his reign by making it his basic orientation, being ready to lose all for the sake of it, or to share his goods with the needy. Nor did Jesus himself envision that the disciple should embrace material poverty as a religious value, still less as an ascetical means. What Jesus himself did, in fact, embrace was the condition of uprootedness proper of an itinerant prophet, with all the painful consequences that involved. And this is what he proposed to his disciple-collaborators (Mt 8:18–22 = Lk 9:57–62).

On this basis, in apostolic Christianity a spirituality of the "poor of the Lord" developed. Throughout the Gospel of Matthew, the poor are those who put their faith and love in God. The poor have the same meaning in the infancy accounts collected by Luke (Lk 1—2). Now the new people of God are the remnant of which Zephaniah spoke. In 2 Cor 8:9, Paul, exhorting the Corinthians to be generous with the poor of the Jerusalem community, offers them as a motive the example of Christ, who "though he was rich, yet for your sake he became poor, so that by his poverty you might become rich." Here we have an idea (though with the added note of generosity) similar to that of the kenosis in the hymn of Phil 2:6–11. This is a radical interpretation of the spirituality of Jesus and his disciples, as a life of generous renunciation on behalf of the needy.

All of this needs to be set against the social background of Israel in the time of Jesus. The general situation was bleak. In his political reorganization of Palestine, Pompey, who had subjected Judea in 63 B.C., had deprived the Jews from the coastal cities and the Decapolis, greatly limiting commerce and impoverishing farmers. Herod the Great confiscated considerable tracts of fertile land and sold them to the richest families. Agrarian properties were in the hands of a few, and this gave rise to a host of dependent fieldworkers. The tariffs imposed by the Herodians and the Romans were felt as a grave burden, causing yet more poverty and pitting the people against the Romans and their collaborators. On top of all this, there were periodic droughts. When Jesus spoke of the poor and announced the imminence of their liberation, he was addressing the great impoverished masses of his people. All of this, it should be noted, had political resonances, whether or not Jesus intended them. Although he proclaimed the message of the kingdom to all, he addressed himself preferentially to all those who were oppressed. This led him to lay particular stress on his ministry to the publicans who, although they had money, were nevertheless at the head of the list of those who were considered by the theology of the day to be beyond hope of pardon. But there came a time when Jesus saw that only the humble, the ignorant and the poor were accepting his message, while the "wise" rejected it (Mt 11:25–26). Jesus found himself at the forefront of the great masses of the poor. He was truly the prophet who had come to proclaim glad tidings to them. The masses wanted, so it seems, to make him king, so that he could lead an uprising against the Romans. But Jesus rejected this. His mission was to proclaim the in-breaking of the divine kingdom. Clearly, to judge from some of his parables, he believed that God did not need anyone to force his hand.

Jesus was left alone with the poor, the great mass of oppressed and outcast people. It was they who received him with joy in Jerusalem, and this must have aroused the fears of the collaborationist clergy (Jn 11:47–54). Shortly afterward, he carried out the prophetically symbolic action of cleansing the temple. The higher clergy handed Jesus over to the Romans.

WHY PROFESS POVERTY?

What does all this have to do with the complete divestment of everything practiced by the first monks and nuns, or with the vow of poverty that the friars began to make toward the end of the twelfth and the beginning of the thirteenth century? Absolutely nothing—or else a great deal, depending on how you look at it. Clearly, the interpretation given poverty from the time of Origen to that of Thomas Aquinas had more to do with a trait common to Hellenistic philosophies than with the Gospel, because among the pagan philosophers, poverty was a condition for the pursuit of wisdom: before a candidate embraced a philosophical career, he was obliged effectively and radically to abandon all material goods. This denudation would allow him to progress in the contemplation of immutable, i.e., divine, being. Socrates proposed, as the ideal, to be like the gods, who needed very little. This was further radicalized at a later date, when material interests came to be considered as trash and as an impediment. Greek poverty was, then, a statement of superiority, and it lay enclosed within the horizons of the individual.

We said above that Origen interpreted Mt 19:21 ("If you would be perfect, go, sell what you possess and give to the poor . . .") in the sense which seemed obvious in his culture: the renunciation of material goods must be for Christians, as it had been for the pagans, the first step toward perfection. Jesus had proclaimed the urgency of the kingdom which was near at hand, and the need to put the demands of the kingdom above one's own life (family, goods), in order to devote oneself to pre-

paring others for the great event. He reminded all that riches could en-
snare them and harden their hearts, so that they would remain outside.
Matthew, in redacting the story of the call of the rich young man, meant
to say the same thing when he wrote: if you would be perfect, go, sell,
give to the poor and follow me. Matthew was not referring to the life
actually led by the disciples, but to the fact that conversion to Jesus (if
you would be perfect) supposes an adherence to him above all else. From
Origen on, however, this began to be interpreted as meaning: if you
would arrive at the personal maturity and perfection that the philosophers
regard as the goal to be gradually arrived at, and which we know can be
found only in communion with Christ, then begin to divest yourself as-
cetically of all material goods, because poverty will purify you and help
you to contemplate. Here, the poor were no longer necessary, although
the spirit of the gospel would often call them to mind. The important
thing was to despoil oneself and renounce all. This, as can be seen, has
little to do with the original sense of poverty in the Gospel. The two
points of view are very different.

But was this the real or complete meaning of the gesture made by
the first monks and later by the mendicants and the members of the various apostolic institutes? We doubt it. Recall that, as we said above, the
definitive meaning of historical facts is not given by the intention of their
authors, but rather by the manner in which they are inserted in their historical context. And history seems to tell us that the renunciation of
goods has always been in the nature of a protest, or at least of a prophetic
counter-proposal. The renunciation made by Antony, Macrina, Basil
and Hilarion was the occasion of such great surprise, because the Church
in their day was becoming a prestigious and powerful institution, which
would end by being assimilated into the empire. The primitive communities were made up of the urban middle class, and this class was now
upwardly mobile, with a full spectrum of possibilities open to it. They
soon began using the term *pagani* (villagers or country folk) to designate
non-believers. The Fathers also speak of the comfortable life being
adopted by the clergy. Thus the monks, in stepping outside the social
network by their renunciation of property, were proposing a type of life
that embodied the transcendent values of the Gospel. They became poor
like the poor and, in some way, with the poor. It should be noted that
the poor were totally absent from the theory of poverty embraced by the
pagans. For the latter, the important thing was to leave their riches be-

hind, ceding them to family or friends, or destroying them. Christians, on the contrary, willed them to the poor who represented Christ (Basil), and, later, not a few of them sold their products in the local market and distributed among the poor whatever was not necessary for their own very austere life.

Likewise, Pachomius and Mary, Macrina and Basil, and, above all, Augustine wanted, through the sharing of goods, to revive the memory of paradise and of the original Christian community. The communities founded by these men and women, and, later, those communities that followed the Rule of St. Benedict, regarded their sharing of goods and the preparatory divestment of their members as a sign whereby they reminded the whole Church of the central value of solidarity. This had its inconveniences when communities eventually became rich and economically powerful. This already happened in the communities of Pachomius (fourth-fifth century). The connection with the poor was lost. And the poor looked with envy on the comfort and security of the cenobites.

For this reason Francis and Clare, and after them the other mendicants, returned to a radical poverty. The Church was then caught between a dying feudal society and a nascent bourgeoise for whom money and property counted more than anything else. This transition impoverished not a few artisans. Numerous poverty movements had arisen to remind the Church of its vocation, and many of them had ended in separation from Rome. The mendicants brought with them a new model of Church: the Church of the poor. But what is more interesting for us is that they decided to be poor *with* the poor. Someone may object that it was conformity with the Gospel, rather than solidarity with the needy, that moved Francis. But it should be noted that the earlier movements of the poor of Christ had been finding their binding force in a return to the Gospel.

This interpretation of poverty, despite its ups and downs in the Church, left a deep mark on the ensuing forms of the religious life. A number of institutes added silent and self-denying work with the humblest classes, especially those for whom there was no place in society. Finally, in our times, the Little Brothers and Sisters of Jesus have returned to being poor among the poorest by means of a silent and pervasive communion of presence. And the religious life in general has come to regard being alongside the poor and fighting for their rights as a central part of its profession of poverty. All of this, on different levels and with different nuances, has truly reached down to the bedrock connection between evil and poverty in the proclamation of the kingdom, as Jesus understood it.

POVERTY, A COMMON CHRISTIAN CALLING

When a religious publicly professes poverty, the reference is to a particular form of Christian poverty, because, understood not simply as a material situation imposed and suffered (which is always an evil in the Bible), but rather as an attitude of faith/hope in the kingdom, whereby a person is oriented toward this kingdom above all material things, then poverty is not just the vocation of a few Christians or an evangelical counsel or a charism: it is unquestionably the vocation of every disciple. The accounts of the call whereby the disciples left all to follow Jesus are aimed at telling us about the common Christian vocation. The same is true of the saying apparently coined by Luke: "So, therefore, whoever of you does not renounce all that he has cannot be my disciple" (Lk 14:33).

What are the implications of this poverty that is part of the vocation of every disciple? It means not just being prepared to lose one's good out of fidelity to the Gospel (although this might have been in the mind of those who repeated the accounts and sayings), but, positively, to orient one's whole life toward the kingdom of divine grace, accepting the message of Jesus in faith. Poverty, as an attitude, is before all else faith and trust in God, accepting his word, acknowledging our total dependence on him as creatures, and our frailty as sinners. This is what makes the persons who appear in the first chapters of Luke to be poor according to the Spirit. At one and the same time, Jesus lays great stress both on liberty of heart ("You cannot serve God and mammon"—Mt 6:24) and on trust in God's providence ("Do not be anxious. . . . Look at the birds of the air. . . . Consider the lilies of the field . . ."—Mt 6:25–34).

But it would be overlooking an essential aspect of this poverty in spirit (Mt 5:3) if we failed to mention the essential relationship that exists between this form of poverty and the kind of poverty that is imposed and suffered. Jesus soon encountered the latter kind of poverty, not only because he addressed his proclamation of the kingdom mainly to the poor and the outcast, but also because he observed that it was the poor and the ignorant who accepted his message, so that he was thus becoming the prophet of the poor. His banquets with publicans and public sinners not only proclaimed the arrival of the kingdom of grace, but were also expressions of solidarity with these people. The country meal that Jesus organized near the lake was not only a dramatized parable of the messianic banquet, but also an expression of the compassion of Jesus (Mt 14:14; 15:32). The preaching of the apostles and apostolic men made the presence of the poor, if one may say so, even more explicit. In the account of the calling of the rich young man, the essential point is, as in the other vocation accounts, to leave all and follow Jesus. But Mark adds "and give to the poor" (Mk 10:21), while Luke changes it to "and distribute it among the poor," thus making it an act of ecclesial communion or sharing (Lk 18:22; cf. Acts 4:35). In the parable on the last judgment, the ones who enter the kingdom of God are those who fed, gave drink to and clothed the poor, and who visited the sick and those in prison (Mt 25:34–40), while the ones who remain outside are those who closed their hearts to solidarity with the poor and afflicted. Recall that Saint Paul, in order to exhort the Corinthians to solidarity with the poor, reminds them that Jesus became poor in order to enrich them by his poverty (2 Cor 8:9).

WITHOUT PROPERTY

The foregoing is the poverty—the common Christian poverty—which religious profess: faith in God, the acknowledging of our dependence and moral misery, confessing that God is our good, trust in him and solidarity with the poor. But religious have, moreover, come to commit themselves to live *sine proprio,* without property, as the rules of the Trinitarians, the Friars Minor and the Poor Clares put it. This is what the monks did from the beginning, and what was later demanded of all candidates to the monastic community before they were incorporated into it: *diappropriatio,* or the self-divestment of everything. The religious performs in public a symbolic act, the content of which is the common poverty of the Gospel, but expressed here in a radical way. This profession, as a parabolic action, reminds the whole Church of its common calling: None of you can be my disciple unless you renounce all your possessions (Lk 14:34). What secular Christians will have to live through in each of the decisions that affect their lives (career, enjoyment of goods, political options), the religious chooses to express by this radical gesture of renunciation.

In promising to live without property, religious realize that they are renouncing a right that comes to them from their Creator, but they also know that it is a right which the vast majority of people do not enjoy. In this way, religious descend to the humiliating condition of the poor. Here, as in the Bible and in the mind of Jesus, material poverty is an evil. Religious, like Jesus, put themselves alongside the poor and the outcast, and renounce the common ideals of power, security and comfort. For this reason, any form of poverty which does not have an essential relationship with the poverty that is suffered by others cannot be a form of religious poverty. Paul VI began his reflections on religious poverty precisely by asking us to listen to *the cry of the poor*.[1] Religious have now found a new, overtly political, way of being alongside the poor: by defending their rights against the powers that be. And they have done and are doing so, not only in the third world, but also, constantly, in the northern hemisphere, through declarations, boycotts, elections, and interventions in banking practices.

In reality, there are material, although not affective, limitations in this identification with the poor. Therefore, religious have to avoid "playing the game" of being poor. For the fact is that everywhere today, especially in highly industrialized societies, an individual's education is his or her best guarantee for tomorrow. Today, few depend on what they inherit from their parents; their best hope for the future lies in getting a university education. And education or instruction is not an external good that can be taken away from us; rather, it is an internal good that affects us intimately and deeply. Nowadays, the really poor are the illiterate or those who have had to leave school in the lowest grades. The poor, in capitalist countries, do not ordinarily attend universities, nor do they have enough money to attend courses, seminars and conferences as most religious do. But in reality, this is not what counts. Religious, in professing poverty, stand alongside the poor in love, make themselves one with them affectively and place all their educational resources at the service of the needy. If these educational advantages are mainly or more commonly the source of personal security and power, religious renounce the fruits of those advantages by promising to live *sine proprio:* I am not going to seek my own security and prestige through my education. I am going to put it, that is, put myself, at the disposal of the poor and needy. To profess poverty *sine proprio* is to commit oneself to live and die for others, especially the most needy. In this sense, poverty is much like celibacy, except that celibacy is realized on the level of interpersonal relationships, while poverty is realized in relationship to things.

COMMUNION OR SHARING OF GOODS

The profession of poverty made by a hermit, or by one committed to celibacy in solitude, even while living in a city, ends there. Men or women solitaries decide for themselves how they are going to procure their own sustenance and how they will use the goods they need. But those who enter a community not only renounce private property, but declare that they are entering into a common sharing of goods with the other members of the community. This involves giving up the ability to appropriate earnings from their own work or from gifts, and that they commit themselves to giving the community an account of the way they use its goods. None of these things is essential for poverty: the anchorites of old did not include it in their profession, despite the fact that they were really poorer than the cenobites; neither do today's hermits and solitaries include it in their profession. But it is very important for a life of communion and therefore for the experience of poverty in community. In the "old system," this was achieved by living in total dependency on the superior. Today we understand and more frequently live it by being responsible before the community for our use of goods. The forms have changed, but so has the social system, which now often requires a greater freedom of movement. From yet another point of view, this is also a consequence of the recent emergence of the person, as a responsible agent, in religious community. For this very reason, since the former kind of total passivity has happily gone its way, co-responsibility needs more than ever to be reinforced.

But all of this supposes that the community as such lives poverty and presents itself, as a group, in solidarity with the poor. Simply being responsible never converted anyone into a truly poor religious. Karl Rahner affirmed this not too long ago: no one can be poor if he or she belongs to a rich community.[2] We should note, however, that the concrete experience of poverty in various religious families depends on their own distinctive charism. There are communities and institutions which profess, so to speak, to dissolve themselves among the masses of the poor in order to carry out a service of presence within them. And there are numerous apostolic institutes which frequently administer large sums of capital in their apostolic works in service of the poor. In the latter case, the religious are, at least theologically and spiritually, administrators in the name of and in the service of the poor. They have to avoid the danger of allowing the level of their lifestyle to be influenced by these goods, and this requires great fidelity to their own vocation and at the same time a constant process of collective discernment. The difficulty is all the greater in rich societies, because the outward environment tends to influence us deeply and to multiply our needs. This last-mentioned problem, however, can be avoided only to a certain point, because the concrete experience of poverty is different in different societies. This was recognized in the decree *Perfectae Caritatis*.[3] But even in the richest countries, poverty requires not only simplicity of life, but also openness to the sufferings of the poor in other places. For planet earth, as the saying goes, has now become a global village.

Notes

1. *Evangelica Testificatio,* n. 17.

2. K. Rahner, ''Theology of Poverty,'' in *Theological Investigations,* VIII, pp. 172, 201.

3. PC 13.

Bibliography

L. Boff, *God's Witnesses in the Heart of the World* (Chicago: CCRS, 1981) pp. 95–115.

A. Cussianovich, *Religious Life and the Poor* (Maryknoll: Orbis, 1979) pp. 1–20.

D.M. Knight, *Cloud by Day, Fire by Night* (Ottawa: Canadian Religious Conference) 1979. Volume II.

F.J. Moloney, *Disciples and Prophets* (New York: Crossroad, 1981) pp. 85–99.

———, *A Life of Promise* (Wilmington: M. Glazier, 1984) pp. 18–73.

Poverty. The Way Supplement 9. Spring 1970.

D. Reese *et al., Consider Your Call* (Kalmazoo: Cistercian, 1980) pp. 205–220.

J. Ridick, *Treasures in Earthen Vessels: The Vows* (New York: Alba House, 1984) pp. 3–25.

IX | A Community of Disciples

When we move on from celibacy and poverty to other themes of the religious life, we note at once that we have passed from common elements to traits that differentiate the various forms of religious life. This was already apparent when we dealt with the theme of community, where we saw the monachate, despite later stress on community, come into being precisely as an eremitical life, which was long considered the highest form of monastic life. In our days, the new Code of Canon Law has returned to a full acknowledgement of the solitary life. And, going beyond the religious life in the canonical sense, the members of secular institutes do not make a commitment to live in community. Here, however, we touch on a differentiating point as regards obedience. Although the new Code requires hermits to make a commitment of obedience to their bishop, it is obvious that a solitary's experience of obedience is quite different from that of members of religious communities. We will treat of this later.

In this chapter we are going to deal with community, and then, in the following chapter, with obedience, both because the practice of obedience arose precisely among the first communities of monks and nuns and because the commitment of obedience is, as we shall see, a commitment to life in community. The religious life has traditionally come to be identified with life in a celibate community, so much so, in fact, that the Latin Code of 1917 passed over the solitary life without even a nod. In the new legislation, life in community has become a factor distinguishing religious from members of secular institutes.

This is a theme of great importance because, during recent years, we have been witnessing a profound transformation of community life. The primarily disciplinary concept of community, imposed mainly in the nineteenth century, has disappeared and given way to a different idea of community founded on dialogue and participation. Gone, too, is monolithic uniformity, so dear to the legislators and rubricians of Romanticism, to be replaced by unity within pluralism. Not a few structures have disappeared in order to allow for personal accords—which have not always been reached. Today's religious are more exposed and vulnerable. Some who sought the security of a structured life now find themselves bereft of it. It is therefore necessary for us to formulate some fundamental questions on the meaning and value of the community life of religious.

JESUS, COMMUNION, COMMUNITY

Let us begin by attempting to relate the theme of religious community to the original experience of Jesus. It is significant that throughout history, in their attempts at self-understanding, religious communities have almost constantly harked back to the model of the apostolic Church of Jerusalem and, much more rarely, to the prophetic group made up of Jesus and his men and women disciples.

The kingdom of God—the core of Jesus' message—undoubtedly had a social aspect. The definitive people of God was going to be established. Like the rabbis, and perhaps with greater insistence, Jesus referred to the future kingdom under the image of a banquet. Even more significantly and typically, he not only spoke of this banquet, but acted it out in the parabolic gesture of eating and drinking with publicans and sinners. But the message of Jesus dealt first and foremost with personal dispositions toward God and toward the in-breaking kingdom. Above all, Jesus spoke to persons and about persons: "Be converted . . . believe . . . be prudent yet simple . . . be merciful . . ." His was an ethical message with roots sunk deeply in the relationship between the person and God. This was the most pressing issue of all. But besides this, Jesus also insisted, as an essential part of his message, on the establishment of right relationships between human persons—relationships inspired by the prior gracious and generous initiative of God: love of neighbor, forgiveness, almsgiving.

From another point of view, the community was, for Jesus, *all Israel*. It was not a matter of elites or separatist groups. Whereas the reigning theology of the day condemned most common folk as sinners, and while the Qumran community set itself apart as an elite of the perfect, Jesus, in contrast, regarded the true community (the Qahal, the assembly of God) as being made up of all Israel. This was the context in which he carried out his mission, which was to prepare all Israel, beginning with the most abandoned, for the definitive salvation-event.

But in order to facilitate the carrying out of this mission, Jesus chose to associate with him a group of men and women disciples. This group was united around the compelling person of Jesus, whose expectations they shared. The men of the group took part in his general ministry of proclaiming and healing, while the women must have done much the same toward other women. One of these women, Mary of Magdala, would later play a decisive role in calling the disciples together again, after their dispersal, following the crucifixion. During the lifetime of Jesus, the group was doubtless supported by some well-to-do widows (single or married women were unable, according to the law, to dispose of their wealth). It was, then, an unusual group, and a prophetic one. Its members had no fixed, common abode, although they were frequently taken in as guests at neighboring homes. It was an open, evangelizing community, which Jesus regarded as his eschatological family. Once, when he was told that his family was looking for him, he told his listeners that his real family were those who did God's will. Mark tells us that as Jesus said this, he pointed to those seated about him, that is, to his disciples. Here, ''doing God's will'' obviously did not have the same legalistic meaning it had among the Pharisees, not only because that would have excluded the majority of Israel, but also because it would have been blatantly contradicted by the practice of Jesus, who dealt preferentially with the marginated. For Jesus, ''doing God's will'' meant accepting the good news of God's imminent intervention in history, and preparing for that intervention. This was the faith/hope that held his group together. And it was a very flexible group. Jesus did not organize rituals for them, or order them to say certain prayers, as the Pharisees and the followers of John the Baptist (Lk 11:1) or the Qumran sectarians did. Neither did he prescribe any special fasts for them (Mk 2:18), or parcel out certain offices among them. What united them, rather, was the expectation, the ministry and, increasingly each day, the person of Jesus.

LOVE AMONG THE DISCIPLES

It was precisely when Jesus had been crucified and lifted up into the glory of God that the disciples began to experience a deeper communion with one another. What united them now was their faith in the risen Lord and their hope in the (imminent) return of the Son of Man. In this way, the first communities of disciples, churches of God in Christ, came into being and, together with prayers they had received from Jewish tradition, began to develop the practice of celebrating the Lord's supper. Naturally, the fact that they were a minority in Israel, and soon afterward, in the Empire, gave them an even closer cohesion.

The social aspect of Jesus' message also underwent further development. Mercy and compassion were stressed, as can be seen in the tradition developed in Matthew's parable of the judgment of the nations, where those who practice solidarity with the poor are declared worthy of the kingdom of God (Mt 25). Similar texts can be found not only in Judaism, but also in Egyptian and Persian literature. The distinctively Christian touch is the discovery of the Messiah, hidden in the poor (Mt 25:34–39). Coinciding with this point of view is the passage in the Letter of James, which declares: "Looking after orphans and widows in their distress and keeping oneself unspotted by the world make for pure worship without stain before our God and Father" (Jas 1:27).

Paul had already worked out a whole theology of love. Love is poured forth in our hearts by the Spirit (Rom 5:5) and is the fruit of the Spirit (Gal 5:22). The whole law is summed up and fulfilled in the command to love the neighbor (Gal 5:14; Rom 13:10). This love is directed toward all, but above all to those with whom we share the faith (Gal 6:10). In his letters to the various communities, Paul constantly stressed that Christians maintain mutual relationships of companionship, marked by generosity, humility and love (1 Cor 13:4–7; Gal 5:25–6:10; Col 3:32; Eph 4:1, 32; Phil 2:1–5). Matthew develops the theme of the style of relationships proper of a community of disciples: authority should not be characterized by lording it over others; leaders should consider themselves devoted to service (20:25–28), one must foster an attitude of religious respect for the little ones (18:5). The Lukan and Johannine Gospels incorporate this exhortation to service in the farewell testament of Jesus at the Last Supper (Lk 22:24–30; Jn 13:3–17).

In fact the Johannine writings carry this notion much further. What distinguishes the disciples of Jesus—the new commandment—is precisely their love for one another. This is the innermost core of Jesus' testament to his Church (Jn 13:33–35; 15:12–15; 1 Jn 2:7–11; 3:14–24; 4:7–8, 11–13, 19–21). Note that the Johannine perspective is not properly one of communion as the foundation of community, but rather that of the relationship between one individual and another. John not only sums up Christian ethics as faith in Christ and love of the neighbor, but goes beyond this by attaching a metaphysical meaning to love. God loves us, and his love reaches us by way of his Son. Love is a heavenly, divine reality which gives us life and enables us to love the neighbor. In John, the verb "to love" is often found without an object, as if to indicate a reality inherent in the lover, rather than a relationship. In fact, one who does not love is dead (1 Jn 3:15; cf. 3:18; 4:19).

COMMUNION: FROM PAUL TO LUKE

We have already observed Paul's statement that love must be given in a special way to those who are of the household of the faith (Gal 6:10). His insistence on solidarity among Christians is well known. They are members of one body in Christ (1 Cor 12:12–27; Rom 12:4–6), because the same Spirit has been poured forth on all of them (1 Cor 12:13). Hence the various ministries and the charisms that dispose us for them are given for the upbuilding of the community (1 Cor 12:5–6, 28–31). In the Letter to the Ephesians, the Church has become the very body of Christ (Eph 1:23). One should also note the determining role that the Eucharist plays in the creation of this ecclesial communion: the cup and the bread signify solidarity with the blood and body of Christ. "Because the loaf of bread is one, we, many though we are, are one body, for we all partake of the one loaf" (1 Cor 10:17).

All of this is possible because, in Christ, God has reconciled us with himself (2 Cor 5:18–19; Rom 5:10). This reconciliation with God appears as the cause of the reconciliation of all. All, whether Jew or Greek, slave or free, have been baptized to form one body (1 Cor 12:13). There is, then, no longer Jew or Greek, slave or free, male or female (Gal 3:28).

In Acts, Luke, more than any other writer of the Christian Testament, makes ecclesial communion to be the distinctive trait of Christian existence. The three summaries (Acts 2:42–47, 4:32–35 and 5:11–15), whereby Acts describes the life of the primitive Jerusalem community, center everything on the communion of its members. In 2:42–47 Luke tells us how all were devoted to instruction, communal life, the breaking of bread and the prayers (2:42), and goes on to explain: "Day by day, attending the temple together and breaking bread in their homes, they partook of food with glad and generous hearts" (2:46). As for their material goods, they "shared all things in common. They would sell their property and goods, dividing everything on the basis of each one's need" (2:44–45). This theme appears with even greater force in the second summary, according to which "The community of believers were of one heart and one mind. None of them claimed anything as his own; rather, everything was held in common . . . nor was there anyone needy among them, for all who owned property or houses sold them and donated the proceeds. They used to lay them at the feet of the apostles to be distributed to everyone according to his need" (4:32–35). The third summary deals with community meetings (5:12b) and growth (5:14). Both the first and the third summary deal with the spread of the Church (2:43; 5:13).

According to Luke, then, the primitive Church lived in a total communion of spirit and goods. This is obviously an idealized picture of things, as we learn from the Book of Acts itself, in the story of how the Hellenists soon had to complain about discrimination against their needy members (Acts 6:1). We should perhaps dismiss the case of Ananias and Sapphira (Acts 5:1–11), which may have been an isolated instance. But on the other hand we might ask why, if everyone really sold his or her goods and pooled the proceeds, we are told about this—that Joseph/Barnabas, the Levite of Cyrus, sold his farm and gave the proceeds to the apostles (4:36–37).

Perhaps we see the hand of Luke the redactor here as he revises and inserts different materials and points of view from his various sources. It seems, for example, that a targum on Dt 5:14, "But there will be no poor among you," reveals a tendency to interpret this as a prophecy concerning messianic times. In this case, Luke was affirming the messianic character of the new community. But contacts with Hellenistic culture and literature seem to be even greater here. Diogenes Laertius, for example, cites a saying of Pythagoras, "Among friends, all is common property"[1]—a saying which became a popular proverb.[2] Indeed, in the *Nicomachean Ethics,* Aristotle had already commented on it: "And rightly so, since friendship consists in sharing.''³ Not only that, but the Stagirite cites alongside it another proverb: Friends are ''as it were, but one soul.'' Epicurus, reacting against the city-state, proposed the foundation of small communities based on friendship. Indeed, Pythagoras imposed the communion or sharing of goods in an attempt to revive the myth of the Golden Age, when all were supposed to have enjoyed the goods of this world, without any hint of ''mine or thine.'' A text from the *Life of Pythagoras* by Jamblichus (d. 330) tells of the Pythagorean community's sense of having ''one single soul,'' of their being loath to use the word ''my,'' and of their having all things in common and not having anything as individual property. The coincidence with Acts is striking.⁴

It is fitting for us to insist on the fact that these traditions concerning the communion of spirits and goods related to the primitive human community. That is to say, they were using the myth of the Golden Age in order to remind their contemporaries of what a truly human society ought to be. Myths of origins often point to values that are fundamental for a society. Acts offers us the myth of the original Christian community: it is telling us what a Christian existence should be, namely, an existence in full communion or sharing. It should be noted that Origen,⁵ and more systematically Cyprian,⁶ had perceived the value of these Lukan summaries: in former times we used to live in fraternal communion, whereas now we are divided. The original communion was recalled in order to upbraid the evils of the present.

PRIMITIVE CHURCH AND RELIGIOUS COMMUNITY

In this context of the myth of the primitive communion of the human race, which the Pythagorean and Neoplatonic communities wished to revive, and in that of the nostalgia for paradise lost that some of the Fathers felt acutely in the third century, it is highly significant that the first religious communities (fourth century) should have returned precisely to these summaries in Acts as their source of inspiration. The Pachomian community (the first known) came to put communion at the center of what we now call the religious life, citing the summaries from Acts to that effect. The larger rules of Basil cite Acts 2:45 three times and Acts 4:32–35 four times, and these seven citations appear, in turn, in the brief rules. For St. Augustine, communion of hearts and goods sums up the whole rule of life of his "monks." He says so clearly at the beginning of his *Praeceptum*. In the rule of Benedict (560 A.D.), this model is less visible, with only two citations on the sharing of goods. This is doubtless due to the stress on individual perfection which he had received from the Master and ultimately from the desert tradition.

Cassian (ca. 420 A.D.) had already theorized on the relationships between the monachate and the primitive Church. Eusebius and Sozomen had still earlier stated that the monks had meant to revive the life of the primitive Church. Cassian gives us two versions of a legend in order to explain this. According to the Alexandrian version, Mark, the bishop of Alexandria, was alleged to have founded a separate community which followed the rule of the first Christians adding to it a rule of sexual abstinence.[7] According to the Jerusalem version,[8] the monachate came into being when the primitive fervor of the Church had decayed and a few good men decided to reestablish it. Christian cenobitism, Cassian tells us, is the continuation of the primitive Christian community. No one should fail to grasp the great importance of all this for an understanding of the vocation of the religious community within the Church.

From Augustine, the use of the image of the apostolic Church as the source of inspiration for a life publicly committed to the service of God later passed on into the clerical communities (the Canons Regular) that came into being as part of the reform of the tenth and eleventh centuries. Significantly, the mendicant orders were to break with this tradition. The reason for this break was that the former model was seen through the monastic and canonical experiences of religious life, in which the communion or sharing of goods often presupposed a certain wealth. This model would reappear, with its full force as an inspirational myth, in some clerical communities founded after Trent. With the revival of sensitivity to community values that developed throughout our own century and has spread strongly in the wake of Vatican II, the texts of the summaries of Acts have been introduced into several revised constitutions, ordinarily in a fundamental chapter on the theology and spirituality of life in communion.

THE VARIOUS THEOLOGIES

It should not be thought that religious communities, throughout these eighteen centuries, have given one single interpretation of themselves. The various theologies of community have depended above all on the experience and teachings of their founders, and these have in turn been conditioned by the social and cultural contexts in which they developed.

(a) Communion, the Central Fact

The Pachomian community seems to have begun out of a functional intention: to help the monks by means of some common structures and spaces. To achieve their end, according to one of the oldest lives of Pachomius, at the beginning they did not profess a total communion of goods, but only contributed partially to sustain the group. But Pachomius had created a common space for them, and this obliged them to relate to one another and to constitute themselves into a community. Little by little, to judge from the texts, a strong spirituality of communion developed among them. Individual asceticism was limited and love was stressed, together with an exaggerated emphasis on common discipline. The Pachomians were called *brothers* and their dwelling places were known as *settlements*. They avoided the vocabulary of solitude. They carried uniformity into all aspects of their life, insisting on the same dress and same quantity of food for all. Not even the person stood out in a singular way. In the beginning, they celebrated the Eucharist on Saturday evenings with the neighboring laity and by themselves on Sundays. Later they isolated themselves. Occasionally they referred to themselves as "the true Israel of the desert." Thus, they understood themselves as a local embodiment of the Church.

Augustine carried this spirituality of communion to its perfection. In his letter to the community of virgins, he tells them plainly that the primary end for which they have gathered together is "to be but one heart and one soul" oriented or moving toward God. Communion is thus the central nucleus of the religious life. Its point of departure and its source of inspiration is the apostolic community of Jerusalem. Augustine cites the summaries from Acts about fifty-three times in his writings. He cites them at the beginning of this letter, then in his *Praeceptum* or rule, and recalls them in sermons 355 and 356, devoted to explaining the kind of common life he had begun with his clergy.[9] Augustine started from a metaphysical concept of love as an inherent reality, rather than as an attitude, and in this he drew his inspiration from John. The uncreated

Love, the divine Spirit, is the One who seals with unity the plurality of Persons in the Trinity.[10] This same Holy Spirit, given at Pentecost, made thousands of souls into one soul.[11] Communion is, then, both a gift of the Spirit and the fruit of a paschal grace, since it is Christ who sends the Holy Spirit into our hearts, thus creating the Church as his body. Augustine discerns two fundamental elements in community: the union of spirits and the sharing of material goods. Relationships within the community are in some way a liturgy. Augustine invites one and all of us to honor God, since we are all his temple.[12] At the same time, Augustine is quite sensitive to the differences between persons. Communion presupposes pluralism and does not suppress it. Rather, he blends both in a higher unity. Note that the two communities that Augustine had organized, first when he was a layman and later as a priest, were centered in themselves, dedicated to prayer and study, whereas the community he founded when he was a bishop united with his priests was open to the rest of the Church in the Eucharist, catechesis and hospitality.

(b) The Gospel in the Center

Basil sees things in another perspective. For him, the important thing is to live the Gospel in its entirety. One must give oneself totally to God through renunciation and leave pagan society.[13] But fraternal communion is an essential part of the Gospel, because God has chosen to crown human sociability with communion. If the first commandment leads us to distance ourselves from the world in order to be faithful to the Gospel, the second calls us to constitute a community.[14] The force that gathered together the members of the communities of Basil and his sister Macrina was, then, the will to live according to the Gospel. However, once constituted, the brothers and sisters of the community sensed at once its wealth and its problematic. For them, the community was above all a system of fraternal relationships. It was through these that one's own charisms were put at the disposal of the rest, that they mutually evangelized one another and practiced the social virtues. Basil saw the community as an actualization of the Church. As soon as he was made a bishop, he would call his brothers to establish a hospital outside the city walls, for the service of pilgrims and the sick. He, too, like Augustine, had to open up to the rest of the Church.

Fraternal communion occupies a similar post in Francis of Assisi.

For him, the important thing was to live according to the Gospel. One is a Friar Minor, in the measure that one is evangelical. But Francis gave himself over to poverty and mobility. His friars would live in the midst of the people and should not lay claim to the ownership of the places they occupy. This meant that, instead of the firmly established communities that had been the rule until then, the accent would now be on fraternal relationships and humble service of one another: "Wherever some of them meet others, the friars should show that they are members of the same family. They should not hesitate to manifest their needs to the others, because if a mother loves her offspring and is concerned for them, a friar ought to love his spiritual brother with even greater tenderness.''[15] The community of Francis was founded, then, on common fidelity to the Gospel and was expressed in relationships of love and humility.

(c) Learning To Serve God

Benedict had already expressed a different concept of community. For him, the monastery was above all a school of divine service. That is to say, the monastic community was founded in order that each of the monks might learn to serve God with his own life. Here, a fundamental value was attached to meditation on the Scriptures, in public or private worship, and in openness to the example and teaching of the leader. The community found its balance in the alternation of prayer and work. A great part of its life was taken up with the liturgy. The monastery was sealed off by cloister and, by that very fact, as a separate community. A number of details reveal that Benedict regarded his community as a local actualization and embodiment of the Church. In fact, although it was enclosed, the monastic community felt itself to be in solidarity with the outside. The rule acknowledges the right of the bishop, of nearby abbots and even of the people, to oppose the taking of possession by an unworthy abbot-elect. The fidelity of the monks to their vocation was therefore important for the whole Church.

(d) Community for Service

In the twelfth century a profoundly new development, part of the revolution then in progress in the religious life, took place: for the first time in history, some communities were founded for an external service to society and the Church—the hospitaler orders. More significantly, however, the beginning of the thirteenth century saw the birth of the Order of Preachers, founded for the preaching of the Gospel. Later, the other mendicant orders included ministry as a fundamental part of their life. In this way the conventual or mixed type of life came into being. In it, religious life was still centered on domestic community observances (somewhat mitigated), but with the important addition of ministries. It was not until the sixteenth century, with Ignatius Loyola, that a fully apostolic community, even as regards observance and discipline, came into being. Since the ministerial needs of the Church had called such institutes into being, it was only right that everything in the community be oriented toward its ministry. External service thus took on an essential value in the way these communities interpreted themselves. They were, in effect, milieus for the development of a form of Christian existence which derived its ultimate meaning from its orientation to an external ministry. They were communities which set their common mission at the center of things, spoke of sharing in the same spirit, and extended the relationships among their members to the ministerial field, either as collaborators in a common ministry, or in a spirit of solidarity with members who worked in different ministries. Choral recitation of the Liturgy of the Hours disappeared, while community meetings and exercises were reduced and were made more flexible.

(e) Women's Communities

The reader may have noticed that we have referred only occasionally to a few women's communities, such as the one founded by Macrina or that of the virgins of Hippo to which Augustine gave his rule. In reality, the foundation of communities for women had been developing along parallel lines with that of men's communities. Mary, the sister of Pachomius, founded a community of sisters on the opposite bank of the river from her brother's foundation. Macrina's foundation preceded that of her brother Basil. Scholastica set up her community near that of her Benedict. Clare of Assisi founded her community shortly after Francis began his movement. Significantly, women's communities were among the first to dedicate themselves to a ministry, mainly that of Christian education. Mary Ward wanted to establish a community that would be as fully apostolic as the one Ignatius had established for men.

We would like to underline a few facts here. In the first place, while the anchoritic life was followed above all by men, with few exceptions, the vast majority of women, from the very outset of monasticism, embraced community life. There were social reasons for this, but perhaps it shows a greater appreciation for relationship on the part of women. Secondly, feminine community has differed little throughout the centuries. Until the sixteenth century, even when the masculine branch of the same order was engaged in ministry, the feminine branch was obliged to follow a purely contemplative life. The reason for this state of affairs was the strict cloister that was imposed on them, thus restraining the initial flexibility that had been enjoyed, for example, by the first Poor Clares. In the seventeenth century, there was a much greater development of women's communities founded for ministries. But in order to pursue these ministries, they either had to forego the canonical form of the religious life (the Daughters of Charity) or else, because of prejudices against a layperson, still less a woman, engaging in a personal ministry, they had to work within the confines of an institution, for which reason most of them ended up following a conventual rhythm of life. It has been only in recent times, above all in the United States, that we have witnessed the emergence of women's communities that are fully apostolic and flexible, centered on interpersonal relationships, rather than structures, featuring personal ministries.

COMMUNITY, AN ESSENTIAL TRAIT

From what has been said, it seems clear that life in community, however differently it is motivated and interpreted, is an essential trait of religious life in the canonical sense, as distinguished from the tenor of life followed in secular institutes. Whether in the monastic life or in those later forms of life oriented toward a specific service (contemplation or an external ministry), religious appear before the Church and society as members of a group of sisters or brothers who profess a communion radically based on the Gospel. As was stated in other terms by Pachomius and Augustine, and suggested by Basil and Benedict, religious aim at actualizing and embodying ecclesial communion in a paradigmatic way.

The Gospel creates both communion and the ecclesial community. Every disciple of Christ lives his or her relationship with God as part of

God's people and as mediated by the community of disciples. The local church, the diocese, is the complete visible incarnation of this communion. Within it, the parish associates Christians in what they have in common: the expression of their faith. But the diocese and the parish, as such, gather in Christ those who are already united socially and culturally, while leaving the faithful dispersed in their various concrete situations. There are fundamentally two Christian communities that bring communion to the level of an interpersonal relationship and create a community of life: the matrimonial community and the community created by the Gospel. The matrimonial community has its ultimate origin in the human reality of love which is consecrated by the sacrament of matrimony. It is a human community taken over by the Gospel. In contrast, what we mean by "a community created by the Gospel" is a type of community which does not have a prior human foundation, but is born of the Gospel. This can be found in two forms, either a secular community or a religious community. In both cases, its members come together in order to jointly show the value of Christian community. Secular communities of this sort, which have appeared with increasing frequency in our times, are communities of single or married Christians who have come together either in order to facilitate their pursuit of particular evangelical ideals of solidarity or in order to share in a common apostolic mission. In contrast, religious communities require their members to commit themselves to celibacy and, in the case of a religious community in the canonical sense, that they also make a public permanent commitment to live in communion.

Naturally, the concrete form of living in communion will differ from one religious group to another, according to their various vocations. Thus, one form will prevail in contemplative monasteries, another in monastic institutes, and yet another in apostolic institutes. But not only communion in the same vocation and spirit, but also the way this communion is expressed in interpersonal relationships is a trait common to all forms of the religious life. Augustine himself stated that the communion of goods, an integral part of religious poverty, performs a function of protest against the selfishness that tends to corrupt society and wound the Church.[16] By gathering together in community, religious repeat in their own lives the parable of the banquet with which Jesus referred to the kingdom of God.

Thus, the community acts as the environment within which religious move and from within which they exert a critical presence before the world and the Church. This is precisely what Cassian meant to say through his two versions of the legend on the origins of monasticism, which claimed that the cenobites continued the lifestyle of the first Christians at a time when the fervor of the Church had grown cold. The fact that Augustine insisted on reviving this ideal of the apostolic Church, after Origen, and, later, Cyprian, had lamented the loss of that primitive communion, is likewise very significant.

COMMUNITY AND CHURCH

In our discussion of the various theological interpretations of religious community, one fact that emerged was that, in most cases, founders viewed their communities as being in some way local actualizations of the Church. This naturally leads to the question: "In what sense does religious community incarnate the Church?"

Above all, it does so in the sense of its being a community of faith. Its members have come together because they have heard the word of God calling them to commit themselves in celibacy, to a particular way of following Christ. And in religious community this word is constantly proclaimed, listened to and meditated upon. Second, because a religious community is constituted precisely as a group of men or women disciples of Jesus, and precisely in order to remind the rest of the Church of the demands of following Christ. In fact, to be a group of disciples is the basic calling of the Church. Third, because religious community is called to express, through charity and the communion of goods, the very reality of the Church. Fourth, because through its very presence and often through its ministries, it is dedicated to the service of the rest of the Church. Lastly, because ordinarily and connaturally, although not necessarily, it is also a community that renders worship to God through public prayer.

But it is quite clear that no community is an ecclesial community unless it is open to the rest of the Church. The local community both incarnates the Church and manifests its solidarity with the rest of the Church. In religious community this is all the more necessary, because it is not a complete local church in that it lacks an episcopate and, in most cases, a presbyterate. Religious communities are situated, in different ways, within a local church presided over by a bishop, and in most cases they must also have recourse to the services of an ordained minister who does not belong to the community.

THE BOND: FAITH/HOPE

There is a passage in the Synoptic Gospels in which Jesus defines the fundamental requisite enabling a group to consider itself to be his family. This is the pericope on the mother and brothers of Jesus in Mk 3:31–35, repeated in Mt 12:46–50 and Lk 8:19–21. On learning that his mother and brothers were outside, asking to see him, Jesus, "looking around on those who sat about him, said, 'Here are my mother and my brothers! Whoever does the will of God is my brother, and sister, and mother.' " It should be noted that in Aramaic there is no single word to designate the family as whole, except for the expression "the house of the father." Here, since Joseph was probably already dead, Jesus had to designate his family by spelling it out as his mother and his other relatives. But the reference was certainly to his family as a whole. The meaning of Jesus' answer is clear. Just as he was asking his disciples to leave behind their families, as he himself had already done, in order to commit themselves to proclaim the reign of God, he had thereby created a new family gathered together by their faith/hope in the coming of that reign. This is precisely what is meant by "doing the will of God."

Applying this passage to the other Christian groups that have been constituted as groups of Jesus' disciples (the Church in its totality, the matrimonial community, the religious community, and the secular community created by the Gospel), we must conclude that a community belongs to Jesus and is bound to him in the measure to which, like him, it stands before God in an attitude of faith. This is how Matthew (who regards the Church as a community of disciples) reinterpreted the Markan passage on the family of Jesus. He rewrote the expression "looking around on those who sat about him," replacing it with "stretching out his hand toward his disciples," in order to indicate that the words of Jesus refer to all those who wish to follow him and not just to the first followers of Jesus (Mt 12:49–50). Luke accentuates this even further by suppressing any concrete allusion and converting the response of Jesus into a general principle: "But he said to them, 'My mother and my brothers are those who hear the word of God and do it' " (Lk 8:21).

Luke confirms our interpretation of "doing the will of God" in Lk

3:35. Entering into communion with God's will means listening to the message of salvation and accepting it for oneself. The contemplative dimension of faith is, therefore, the bond that unites the disciples gathered in religious community. A group of Christians are the family of Jesus, to the extent that like him and with him they place themselves before God, asking themselves about their own meaning, and listening to the word. A group is not Christian above all because it does this or that work, prays more or less, or acts with greater or lesser intensity, but rather because its members live before God, united by faith and hope.

Obviously, we are here touching upon matters of obedience and discernment, essential factors in religious community as they are in every Christian community. We will deal with them in the following chapter.

COMMUNITY: GIFT AND TASK

Augustine often dwelt on the fact that communion and the community which it creates is always the effect of the presence and action of the Holy Spirit, and a gift of the risen Christ, who sends us the Spirit. Human sociability, St. Basil used to say, is thus elevated to the level of a communion. Religious community is a gift because, like every Christian community, it lives on the charity that is poured forth by the Spirit. But it is also a gift because its communion comes into being around a special charism and as the fruit of a vocation.

This always happens when a new religious family is founded, and it continues happening throughout its history, with the incorporation of new members. The community was originally born because some men or women recognized themselves in the charism granted to their founder or foundress, that is to say, they recognized that there was an identity between certain aspects of their own personal vocation and certain aspects of the vocation of the person who was called to found the group. It is the sharing in this vocational gift that creates a communion among certain Christians and leads them to form a community. They feel called by God to form a family in Christ.

This tells us something very important: communion is a divine gift which must be sought humbly and insistently in prayer. This is especially so because our sins threaten this gift continually.

But if communion is a grace, it is a grace that must be actively developed through the cooperation of the members of the community. The community does not exist, spiritually or humanly speaking, by the mere fact that the organization exists, because the community is essentially a network of interpersonal relationships that have to be established, protected and developed. The effort to achieve this is so often very painful, because each member brings to the community not only his or her gifts, but also his or her deficiencies. In some cases, communication and friendship are extremely difficult, for moral or psychological reasons.

PLURALISM AND COMMUNION OF PERSONS

The experience of communion is something that is only gradually achieved in the life of a community, because the point of departure is always a group of persons who are not only united by a common vocation, but are also different from each other. They are different in their gifts and often sharply contrasting in their defects. Even the diversity of their gifts can lead to differences in attitudes and points of view. For in this case we are speaking of a group which, unlike a matrimonial community, is not founded on attraction and complementarity, and is moreover not worked out with just one other person, but with several at the same time.

The presence of defects obliges the members of a religious community (and also members of a family) to be reconciled from time to time. The grace of the sacrament of reconciliation must here be extended to interpersonal relationships, which are often the subject matter of one's confession of faults and failings. From this point of view, community can be seen to exercise a purifying or, if you will, a therapeutic function. Living together constitutes a challenge to selfishness and a call to generosity. In fact, this therapeutic function must go beyond reconciliation. The members of a family, whether religious or matrimonial, are called to the mutual healing of one another's wounds. All bring to the group their tiredness and their crises. And the rest have to have enough strength to help the suffering overcome these burdens, even when they themselves might be undergoing similar difficulties.

Theoretically, the positive side of the picture seems harder to develop, namely, achieving communion from a starting point in a plurality of personalities with their different gifts. It must be borne in mind that religious community, like any other human society, is founded in order to facilitate the full development of its members. This presupposes a climate of freedom. Only a free space will allow for the growth of persons. At times, this seems to have been forgotten in the course of history. The Pachomian rules and regulations imposed a minutely detailed discipline on community members. This was doubtless a consequence of the huge number of brothers—some eight hundred and up—that made up each settlement. The greater the number of members, the greater the difficulty in maintaining interpersonal relationships, and the greater the temptation to adopt a disciplinary approach to living in common. Basil corrected this mistake by asking that each of his fraternities be composed of a few members. The nineteenth century saw the full flowering of a disciplinary concept of community, founded on uniformity and on obedience as a form of self-abnegation. This was the type of community that was destined to disappear after Vatican II.

But community cannot live on liberty alone, because personal responsibility and solidarity with others are equally necessary for its survival and growth. Common ideals must also be preserved and fostered, and among these ideals, communion ranks high. And this presupposes that the members use their own liberty to renounce their own tastes and opinions, for the good of their common task.

A disciplinary community is built vertically, from the top down. In contrast, a community that is the expression of communion in freedom sets a high value on dialogue and the collaboration of all in making important decisions. And this is true quite independently of the various juridical forms of government that exist in different religious communities.

CHARITY AND FRIENDSHIP

Obviously, the minimal experience of living in communion entails respect for personal differences and a common calling. This is, to be sure, something, but it is not enough, because religious have come together in order to experience the mystery of Christian communion.

In this case we are speaking of a love which comes from God and which, by that very fact, partakes of the qualities of divine love, which consist precisely in being creative and, in view of human fallenness, redemptive as well. This means that we must love with a generous love, showing kindness even or above all when we encounter psychological or moral evil. Christian love goes beyond all defects that appear on the surface, in order to discover the divine goodness in the neighbor. It is a love born of a vision of faith. We have already seen how Augustine invites us to worship God in one another, since we are God's temples. Love, therefore, inspires in us an attitude of humble service to one another.

In this context, there is a richly illuminating little story. It seems that once upon a time in a far-off ghetto there lived a group of Orthodox Jews who were famous for their piety and hard work. But as the years went by, the group began to fall off. Relationships soured, the spiritual atmosphere cooled, and work began to lag. The young began to leave. One day, one of the elders called the remaining members together to see what might be done in order to stave off the apparently inevitable end. They decided to take counsel in the matter with a rabbi who was regarded by all as a great servant of God. After several days of prayer and reflection, the rabbi gave them his considered opinion: ''The solution to your difficulties lies in the fact that one of your number is the Messiah.'' The members of the group set about reflecting on this astounding pronouncement. At first, each of them began discounting this or that one among the others, and an occasional individual even entertained the suspicion that he himself might be the Messiah. But little by little, they all began to treat each other with affectionate veneration. ''After all,'' they would think, ''perhaps so-and-so is the Messiah.'' The group came to life again and began to attract new candidates. The hidden Messiah had saved them. In fact, this is a quite Christian story. The parable of the judgment of the nations in Mt 25:31–46 teaches us to serve the Messiah hidden in each of our neighbors, especially in the most needy. In this way love, as Thomas Aquinas said, in some sense becomes a liturgy.[17]

When we speak of charity toward the other members of a community, we are perforce speaking of the love of friendship. As St. Thomas repeatedly observed, charity is friendship, because it is a generous love that seeks the well-being of the other.[18] We can have an inclination to charity toward our neighbor of which we are unaware, but when we are actually dealing with a neighbor with whom we share a common life-experience, charity tends to be converted into human friendship, since it must necessarily be expressed in relationships, in dialogue and in service. Surely, of course, it is not possible to experience true friendship with each and every one of the religious we live with, because there may be very strong psychological obstacles to doing so. But it is indeed possible to have a friendly attitude toward all.

The first step on the road to friendship is mutual respect for differences in personalities, temperaments, sensibilities, ways of relating to one another and ideas. Without respect, no form of love or solidarity is possible. The second step is the establishment of at least a minimum of solidarity with all the members of the group. We must consider all to be equally members of the group, avoiding all those subtle forms of excommunication into which we tend to fall. This means listening to all, trying to support others when nothing prevents us from doing so, etc. The third step is honest communication when we are talking to one another, not only about what we are doing or about what is happening to us, but also about our feelings. Obviously, this kind of communication will grow deeper as our friendship grows deeper. But it can be achieved even with a minimum of respect and solidarity. Finally, we must be concerned for others' feelings and their ills, their joys and sorrows as our own. This in itself is already friendship.

Thomas Aquinas repeated, nevertheless, that charity is a form of friendship *(amicitia quaedam).* He did not say simply that charity is friendship without further precision. The reason is that the New Testament (Paul, Acts, John) presents charity as God's gift infused by the Spirit. Christian love, in God and in God's Christ, tends therefore to reproduce two qualities proper to divine love. First, God loves us with a creative love. God's love, unlike human love, does not fall upon an already existing goodness. Before God loves us, nothing exists. God loves and creates. Christian love must therefore irradiate goodness. In Christ, particularly, God's love appears as a redeeming love. God's love liberates from evil and sin. For that reason, Jesus loved the most needy with a preferential love. Christian charity must therefore become compassion toward those who, *apparently,* are in greater need of love.

Notes

1. *Vita Pythagorae,* VIII, 10.
2. Cicero, *De Offic.,* I,16,15. Seneca, *De Benef.* VII,4,1.
3. *Ethic. ad Nichom.* VIII, 1: 1159b, 31.
4. *Vita Pythagorae,* 167–169.
5. *Comm. Ser.* 35, Matth.: CCS 11, 67–68.
6. *De Lapsis* 6; *De Cath. Eccl. Unit.* 24–26; *De Opere et elemosynis,* 25–26; *Ep.* 5; *Ep.* 7.

7. *De Instit. Coenob.* 2,5.

8. *Conlat.* 18,5.

9. *Precaeptum* I.2: *The Rule of Saint Augustine with Introduction and Commentary* by T.J. Van Bavel (London: Darton, Longman and Todd, 1984) p. 11.

10. *Tract. in Joan.* 14,9: PL 35, 1508.

11. *Inter Op. Maximi Arelat.:* PL 42,715.

12. *Praeceptum,* I.8: *The Rule of Saint Augustine,* p. 13.

13. *Ref. fusius,* Int. 1–2: PG 31,905–915. Int. 6: PG 31,925–928.

14. *Reg. Fusius,* Int. 3.2: PG 31,917; Int. 7: PG 31,929.

15. *Reg.* 1223, c. 6.

16. *Enarr. in Ps.* 131, 5.7: PL 37,1718–1719.

17. 2-2 q 188 a 2.

18. 2-2 q 23 a 1.

Bibliography

H.M. Beha, *Living Community* (Milwaukee: Bruce, 1967).

T. Dubay, *Caring: A Biblical Theology of Community* (Denville: Dimension Books, 1973).

R. Hammett, L. Sofield, *Inside Christian Community* (Paris: Le Jacq, n.d.).

P. Hinnebusch, *Community in the Lord* (Notre Dame: Ave Maria, 1975).

J.M. Lozano *et al., Together Before the Lord: Religious Community Today* (Chicago: CCRS, 1983).

A. Mascolo, *Christian Fraternity and Religious Witness* (Ottawa: Canadian Religious Conference, 1971).

W.W. Meissner, *Group Dynamics in the Religious Life* (Notre Dame: University Press, 1966).

D. Rees *et al., Consider Your Call* (Kalamazoo: Cistercian, 1980) pp. 110–127.

C.J. Van der Poel, *Religious Life: A Risk of Love* (Denville: Dimension Books, 1972) pp. 101–115.

X || Communion in the Will of God

In beginning these remarks on the theme of obedience, we are really doing little more than continuing our reflections on community. Even the first monks realized that while the life of a solitary was characterized by radical poverty, the life of a monk living in community (a cenobite) was distinguished by obedience. In fact, in desert solitude there was no obedience, since there was really no community, except for the initial period when an aspirant strove to learn docility to the teachings of a master, at the end of which he went off as an approved disciple, to search out his own solitude.

PROBLEMS

If the interpretation of chastity has long been burdened with a negative view of sexual relationships, and if the interpretation of poverty has continually oscillated with successive swings of the pendulum of social change, the theology of obedience seems, if possible, to have suffered even more. On the one hand, obedience has very often been understood in terms of a response to orders from an authority—an understanding which greatly restricts the true scope of evangelical obedience. On the other hand, interpreters have occasionally invented ideologies of obedience based on the renunciation of one's own will and judgment. Like all ideologies, these have been aimed at reinforcing institutions or at averting crises. For example, the way in which the author of the *Rule of the Master* stresses the renunciation of the will seems to indicate that he confuses personal free will with "self-will" in the ascetical or moral sense of a desire opposed either to the will of God or to fraternal love. Significantly, when Benedict set about composing his own rule, he omitted the more negative texts from the Rule of the Master. Centuries later, Jansenism, with its reaction against natural human values, strove to equate renunciation of the will with that self-annihilation before the divine Majesty which it inculcated on its own fervent followers. In not a few religious circles, especially after the French Revolution, the very word "liberty" took on a negative connotation.

Besides this, there is the whole vexing problem of making obedience jibe with the Gospel. Those who regarded the annihilation of the person in the sight of God as being the very center of religion have had no problems in this connection. The texts on renunciations made by the disciples were stretched to include the renunciation of their wills, while Jesus himself was made the very model of submission for all the world to see. Meditation manuals insistently reminded us that he was submissive to his parents (as we could all see in Lk 2:31), to the priests, and even to the soldiers who put him to death. Nowadays we would tend to suspect, to say the very least, that Jesus was by no means as submissive as these meditations on obedience would have us believe. In fact, to our way of thinking, he was a quite "difficult" prophet, especially in the presence of the religious hierarchy of his day.

In the past, legislators of the religious life often harked back to one Gospel text in particular as the basis for the duty to obey: "Whoever hears you, hears me" (Lk 10:16). The author of the Rule of the Master went so far as to interpret this text as the basis for the institution of a religious hierarchy of abbots, alongside the ecclesiastical hierarchy of bishops. Others used it to bolster the authority of religious superiors by mystically identifying the latter with Christ. All of these interpretations overlook the fact that the text in question refers to the whole prophetic community of disciples, and not just to its leaders.

Traditionally, under the influence of institutions—which naturally tend to affirm themselves (a sociological law)—the distinction between obedience to God in faith and obedience to a human authority has often been blurred. Nevertheless, the vocabulary of the New Testament is quite enlightening on this point. The term *hypakoe* (obedience), with the one exception of Phlm 21, expresses a religious attitude of faith in God, and the corresponding verb *hypakouein* ordinarily takes God or faith as its object. In contrast, when the reference is to human authorities of any sort, the verb used is *hypotassein* (to be subject to). In our own day, we might translate this in terms of "being accountable or responsible for."

But the problem of obedience is deeper and more serious than this. Jesus was certainly not what we would call an ascetic. We must insist on this, because his message has often been given a one-sided reading. Jesus does not speak of renunciation as a means to individual perfection. He does speak of totally orienting our persons and our lives toward the kingdom of God and of being ready to leave behind anything that might prove to be an impediment to our total fidelity to this commitment. But he attaches no great importance to renunciation as a value in itself. And he surely never portrayed the renunciation of our own will—let alone submission to another human being—as a value.

Yet there has never been anything more deeply evangelical than obedience as Jesus understood and lived it. This is where we must begin: not by projecting our theologies and ideologies on Jesus and the Gospels, but, rather, by humbly reading the texts in their contexts, in an attempt to grasp, as best we can, their original meaning.

"THE WILL OF HIM WHO SENT ME"

Jesus, good Jew that he was, saw God as sovereign and loving. The important thing for him was not to speculate on the nature of God, but to try to discern his will, and thus enter into the blessings of the covenant and the promise. As a lay prophet, he saw religion as being centered in ethics, an ethics of obedience. In some of his sayings, the human person appears as one who owes God total obedience. The will of God is obviously expressed in the Scriptures of Israel, but here we observe a great difference between the attitude of Jesus and that of the masters and the pious of his time. He does not attach equal binding force to all precepts of the law; rather, he counterpoises texts against texts, in an endeavor to search out the underlying divine intention. The granting of a writ of divorce, for example, was concession to human weakness, but God's original intent is revealed in the account of the creation (Mk 10:2–9). The practical interpretation of obligations relating to the sabbath must be deduced from God's original intention in establishing the sabbath (Mk 2:23–28). And within the law itself, justice, mercy and truth are much more important than laws regulating tithes (Mt 23:23–24). This means that not even the precepts of Scripture are "automatic." Jesus repudiates a legalistic mentality in regard to obedience. The human person is called to discern the divine intention underlying the letter of the law.

The concept of obedience to the will of God appears most richly in the preaching of Jesus, where it is set in the eschatological perspective in which Jesus moved. The kingdom, for Jesus, is the manifestation of God's will, a will of grace and salvation. To hear the word, i.e., the proclamation of God's reign, and to do the will of God, are synonymous. One obeys when one accepts this liberating grace. Matthew transmits a saying of Jesus in which he proclaims that "it is not the will of my Father who is in heaven that one of these little ones should perish" (Mt 18:14). Although this saying is not intended as a definition of the will of God in itself, but only as a statement that the loss of his little ones is contrary to God's will, nevertheless the connection of the two is significant.

John generalizes this concept: "For this is the will of my Father, that every one who sees the Son and believes in him should have eternal life; and I will raise him up on the last day" (Jn 6:39–40). Here, we are already in the presence of a theological reinterpretation of the teaching of Jesus on the will of God, as seen in the light of the overall meaning of the life, death and exaltation of the Lord. John describes the whole earthly existence of Jesus as a continual doing of God's will. "He who sent me is with me; he has not left me alone, for I always do what is pleasing to him" (Jn 8:29). "I know him and keep his word" (Jn 8:55). "My food is to do the will of him who sent me" (Jn 4:34). Jesus lived, then, in constant company with him who sent him, listening to his words, that is to say, discerning his loving will, and carrying it out. This interpretation is historically founded on the reality of Jesus' attitude (cf. Mt 11:25–27).

It is significant that while in Matthew Jesus speaks of the will "of my Father" (Mt 7:21, 12:50, 18:14) or "of the Father" (Mt 21:31), and in Mark of the will "of God" (Mk 3:35), he constantly speaks in John (with the single exception of Jn 6:40) of the will "of him who sent me." The will of God and the mission of Jesus are thus closely interrelated. And the will of God is our salvation. We have read it expressly stated in Jn 6:39–40.

What we have here is a truly liberating concept of the will of him who sent Jesus. In it, God is not perceived as a super-patriarch or super-ego who, in some far-off heaven, makes certain decisions or orders certain things to be done, imposing them as a condition for our salvation. This is an oppressive image of God which certain modern thinkers have criticized, either as being linked to psychological oppression (Freud) or as being the source of social oppression (Marx). On the contrary, what God wants is our salvation, and this is also the mission of Jesus. It seems that this liberating idea of God's will is linked in Jesus with his faith in the imminent coming of the divine kingdom, understood as the definitive act of salvation. Jesus was utterly certain that the Father was going to intervene in history, in order to save his sons and daughters.

Later, his disciples would present Jesus as a model of obedience. Thus, Paul would write: "Just as through one man's disobedience all became sinners, so through one man's obedience all shall become just" (Rom 5:19). And the hymn in Philippians would proclaim: "He did not deem equality with God something to be grasped at. Rather . . . he humbled himself, obediently accepting even death, death on a cross" (Phil 2:5–8). Note that in both of these texts, too, the obedience of Jesus is related with our salvation.

OBEDIENCE TO THE GOSPEL

All of these things were expressed in an entirely new way in the wake of the paschal experience, that is, in the experiences that followed the crucifixion-exaltation of Jesus. The salvation willed by God had been manifested in the death and resurrection of his Son. This is the very content of the Gospel preached by the Church. For this reason, the Christian Scriptures often speak to us of "obeying the Gospel" (Rom 6:17; 10:10; 2 Thes 1:8; 2 Cor 10:15; 1 Pt 1:22), of being "obedient to the faith" (Acts 6:7), or of "obeying the word" (2 Thes 3:14). At this time, the accounts of the disciples' calling and prompt obedience were taking shape, and were being proposed to the Church as models of obedience to the Gospel, that is, as models of total conversion to the message and person of Christ.

It is clear that in all these texts, obedience means accepting the plan of God which has been fulfilled in Christ. It is, then, a matter of faith. Nothing is said about obeying a text as if it were a rule of life (after all, the Gospels as such did not yet exist when these texts were first written); rather, we are told to accept the message of our salvation in Jesus, who was crucified and is now lifted up. Throughout the Christian Testament, obedience comes to be synonymous with faith. It is noteworthy, in this connection, that Bible dictionaries and concordances have to oscillate continually between ''faith'' and ''obedience'' when they attempt to translate *hypakoe,* just as they must oscillate between ''infidelity'' and ''disobedience'' to translate *apeitheia.*

OBEDIENCE IN COMMUNION

The rich meaning of Christian obedience does not end here. Its fundamental meaning, certainly, is to accept the fact that God wants to save us here and now. The reign of God means the salvific intervention of God in history, even though this reign will have its culminating manifestation in the beyond. Remember that the healings of Jesus were but the sign and beginning of salvation. God wants us to develop fully as persons, as his sons and daughters. God wants our total well-being. But at the same time, the Christian Scriptures are filled with references to a word which calls us and to a gift that readies us for various types of Christian existence and ministries. Christian obedience is, radically, the acceptance of the Gospel. But at the same time, in a second phase, it is also a discernment of the motions of the Spirit who calls us to a concrete situation where we ourselves can be saved and where we can collaborate with God toward the salvation of others. The lives of the first anchorites begin with an account of their obedience to their vocation, as the concrete embodiment of their call to follow Christ. This sort of obedience is the foundation of the various forms of Christian life and of the various services of matrimony, the single life, the religious life, the ordained ministry, the laity, etc.

Each human person does not look for his or her own salvation while isolated. Faith has set each of us in a situation of communion with others. This is what gives rise to the Church and the various communities within the Church. We already saw, in dealing with community, how Jesus associated with him a group of men and women who shared his hope and collaborated with him in proclaiming it. More than this, Jesus declared that those who (like him and with him) do the will of God are his family (Mk 3:35). A particular group is the family of Jesus or a community gathered around him, to the extent that it stands united before God in order to discern and do his saving will. Obedience, in this deep, evangelical sense, is the bond that unites every Christian community. It is the bond which unites the Church, the community of disciples; it is the bond which unites the matrimonial community of two people standing together before God; it is the bond which unites the various ecclesial communities and, among them, the religious community.

Now we can better understand the meaning of the commitment of obedience that jointly characterizes the members of secular institutes and religious institutes. While the matrimonial community is united by a sacrament that elevates conjugal love, religious and the members of secular institutes make a commitment of obedience in order to form a family in Christ and in his Church. In the former community, there is a sacrament; in the latter, there is an ecclesial commitment. The commitment of obedience makes it possible to belong to this family. These Christians, in response to a vocation, decide that from then on they are not going to make the most important decisions of their life on their own, but that they are going to do so in communion with others.

This means two things. In the first place, obedience is above all obedience to the community. It is a bond of communion with one's brothers or sisters. Obedience to those who have the responsibility to make certain decisions is owed to them precisely because these persons, in virtue of their office, represent the community. Religious authority is born of community and is a service to community. In the second place, this profession of communion entails, as a necessary consequence, the renunciation of the right to make decision on our own, or to follow our own ideas and inclinations. Communion, which brings us so many good things, also demands that we freely sacrifice our own likes and tastes.

This is the meaning of religious obedience: *not* above all that we are called by God to sacrifice the liberty that he has given us and that makes us like him. There is not a hint in the Scriptures that God asks this of us. The God of the prophets and the Father of Jesus does not seek our annihilation. What he does want is that we conform our will with his saving love, thus orienting and enlarging our freedom, but, there is something greater than freedom in isolation, and that something is communion in love, freely accepted. And this in turn demands that whoever decides to enter into communion should freely limit the field of his or her decisions. The object of the commitment of obedience is not to deny or mortify one's freedom but, rather, to live in communion and consequently to forego making isolated decisions, to the extent that this is required for the sake of communion. Through their vow, men and women religious do what Christian spouses do through sacramental celebration—no more or no less.

We have taken our starting point in evangelical obedience—faith in God and in his Christ, the acceptance of his plan of salvation, and communion with others in this faith—in order to arrive at the obedience to which religious and members of secular institutes commit themselves. Let us now fix our attention on the history of the religious life, in order to see how obedience arose in it, as well as the various forms this obedience has taken.

MONASTIC OBEDIENCE: FAITH

In the monachate, obedience has a fundamentally pedagogical or formative function. It is mainly a question of docility, a word which comes from the Latin *docere* and designates the attitude proper of one who wishes to learn through a master. In the desert, docility or openness to the experience and teaching of an elder was a necessary requisite for assimilating the spirituality and rule of life proper of the monachate. Some of these masters refused to give orders, saying, in effect, "Watch what I do." When they did give orders, the orders usually had a pedagogical intent and function.

While obedience, in anchoritism, was a transitory attitude, lasting until the novice was sufficiently prepared to go off into solitude, the situation of obedience became permanent in the *Rule of the Master* and in the Rule of St. Benedict. To be sure, the rule foresaw the possibility that persons proven by long years of living in the *cenobium* might decide to go into the eremitical life, but Benedict regarded it to be the normal case that a monk should remain in the community until death. The community was set up as a school of divine service, presided over by the abbot or, in women's communities, by the mother. The main and essential function of these presiding figures was to teach the monks or nuns the ways of the Lord. The abbot does this, says the rule, by his life and doctrine.[1] In one instance, both the Rule of the Master and that of Benedict relate the obedience of the monk, not to the orders of the abbot, but to his doctrine.[2] The abbot, we are told, explains the commandments of the Lord, although we must bear in mind that the rule, following the monastic tradition, uses the term "commandment" as a synonym for a biblical text.

We are, therefore, dealing with a conception of obedience that is very close to the meaning it has in the Christian Scriptures.

Certainly, the leader of the monastery is also the one who decides on basic norms for the community *(constituere)* and has authority to issue orders *(iubere),* but because community order is essential to the spiritual progress of the individual members. We should note that this is also basically the same function of the leader of monastic or quasi-monastic communities in Buddhism, Jainism and Sufism. Behind all this, there is a profound insight. Religious experience is too rich, and hence too dangerous, for an individual to believe that he or she is capable of cultivating it without consulting others. In a Buddhist monastery, the abbot incarnates the wisdom of the past: in a Christian monastery, he is the representative of tradition. But in the rule of St. Benedict, not even the abbot stands alone. Not only are the Scriptures and the rule above him,[3] but he is also instructed, in important matters, to call on the whole community for counsel. The reason given for this in the rule is very significant: "Because the Lord often reveals the better course to a young monk."[4] For matters of lesser importance, the advice of the community elders suffices. The abbot, too, is called to learn from his community.

Besides this, Benedict added to the end of his rule some chapters on relationships among the monks. It is in this context that he speaks of mutual obedience, probably drawing on Basil as his inspiration. But with this we come to another concept of obedience.

OBEDIENCE AS FRATERNAL LOVE

In the history of the religious life there is another, equally ancient and rich, tradition on obedience. It can already be glimpsed in the communities of Pachomius and Mary, where spirituality was centered on love for one another. The members entered the community out of an intention to live in communion, and not primarily by the desire to learn. This is why most of their exhortations speak above all about charity. The two Pachomian texts that refer to obedience in relation to community discipline remind the members that each has freely chosen to enter community.[5] Starting with the communities of Basil and Macrina, the connection between obedience and fraternal charity appears even more clearly, giving rise to a long tradition that stretches through Augustine to the Canons Regular to Francis and Clare of Assisi, and reaches as far as Ignatius Loyola, Vincent de Paul and the apostolic communities.

Obedience here refers above all to decisions affecting the life of the community and its members, whether as regards decisions already expressly stated in the rule (from Augustine on) or as regards those that are made in practice as the need arises. This type of obedience is required, Basil tells us, both for the solidarity of the brothers and out of a desire to preserve peace within the group. Augustine devotes the greater part of his Letter or *Praeceptum* to charity, stating a number of inspiring principles that others would mention when they dealt with obedience. The reason is that, for him, the real inspiration for the life of a group comes from charity, and authority should intervene only when charity seems to falter. In his commentary on Psalm 99, he says: "Let them love one another, so that their ships may reach port without colliding; but if a strong wind should come up, then a prudent helmsman should intervene."[6] Ignatius Loyola, too, speaking of means to preserve union among the dispersed Company, states: "because this union is brought about in great part, by the bond of obedience . . ."[7]

Precisely because obedience is born of charity, Basil insists on the mutual obedience of the brothers, that is, on their communion of wills, to which he devotes several sections in the first draft of his *Asketikon*.[8] Francis of Assisi, too, asks his brothers to "serve and obey one another in a spirit of charity. For this is the true, holy obedience of our Lord Jesus Christ."[9]

OBEDIENCE IN APOSTOLIC INSTITUTES

The reader will have noticed that, in describing the historical development of this second interpretation of obedience as an expression of fraternal charity, we have cited monastic institutions (the women for whom Augustine wrote his Letter and, in their evolved state, the Pachomians), quasi-monastic institutions (Basil and Macrina), institutions with ministries (the Franciscans), and, finally, institutions founded for the ministry. The fact is that, rather than developing an independent tradition of obedience, apostolic institutes have adopted the vision of obedience as a consequence of a communion of love.

What is distinctive about apostolic institutes is the fact that, since they are so to speak centered outside themselves by their being founded to serve the rest of the Church through external ministries, communion among their members implies that they share the same apostolic spirit and the need to work together in carrying out the mission of the institute. By this very fact, their obedience is above all availability for their common mission. Their members stand before God to confront not only their own individual or collective lives, but also the situation of the Church and society, with the saving will of God.

A quite different matter is the way in which institutes founded during the last four centuries came to develop a type of personal authority tied to vertical structures of government. This turn of events is rooted not so much in the Gospel origins of obedience as in the governance of communities and, hence, in certain practical aspects of obedience. Ignatius Loyola took this direction above all because the dispersed and centrifugal situation in which the first Jesuits lived and worked needed to be counterbalanced by a correspondingly strong centripetal force. Later, at a time when individualism prevailed, community, under the influence of an authoritarian mentality in politics, was understood above all as a disciplinary reality. Now, however, that rugged individualism and political authoritarianism have so to speak fallen from grace, this situation has changed radically, and the fundamental sense of obedience in these institutes has connaturally come to express itself once more as a communion of love through dialogue and participation in decision-making.

EVANGELICAL OBEDIENCE: FAITH AND LOVE

There are, then, in the history of the religious life, two basic traditions, both inspired by the Gospel. The first tradition is above all an expression of faith, born of an attempt to illumine religious experience through the word of God transmitted by human mediation. In this interpretation of obedience, the main stress is on the person as an individual seeking to encounter God in his or her own spiritual progress. This is the monastic tradition which Christianity has in common with other religions. The second tradition is above all an expression of love of neighbor, born of an endeavor to carry the communion of spirits into the praxis of life. In this second interpretation of obedience, the main stress is on the person as existing in communion with others. Whereas the first interpretation speaks of doctrine founded on experience, and of openness and docility to that doctrine, the second interpretation speaks of solidarity, union and peace. They are both forms of expressing communion before God, because both monastic obedience and the obedience of fraternity reveal a communion of Jesus' disciples seeking God's will, and create a community.

But although this distinction is founded on reality, it is also clear that every form of religious obedience, including that of secular institutes, is at once an expression of faith and of charity. Because every evangelical family is essentially a group of disciples gathered around the mystery of divine love, obedience is not only a communion in an attitude of faith before the word of God, but is at the same time an acceptance of human mediation in discerning the will of God. Even in non-monastic fraternities, the individual listens to the community, that is, accepts the collaboration of the rest in the process of discernment. Promising to obey, like getting married, means entering into a communion of faith. Ecclesial communion is brought down from the more general level of the Church's teaching, from which we cannot isolate ourselves, to the concrete level where human life goes on. In turn, however, monastic obedience is also a manifestation of charity. The monk feels solidarity in love with the whole Church, and decides to live this communion in a community. St. Benedict insinuated this when he added his chapters on fraternal relationships and mutual obedience to a rule that speaks above all of docility to the example and doctrine of the abbot. Faith and love, evidently, cannot be separated.

This, then, is evangelical obedience: not a simple response to a norm, a commandment or an order, that is, to a purely juridical and disciplinary reality,[10] but, rather, an habitual attitude of communion with a group and its leaders in faith and in love. It should be noted that obedience, not only as communion in faith but also as communion in charity, has an essential relation with God and his salvific will. Obedience makes the community into a group open to the infinite mystery of God as the loving will who calls to us from the future. It is a radically theological attitude, never a merely sociological reality.

OBEDIENCE: PRAXIS

Naturally, faith must be expressed in some sort of praxis: one must "act in truth," as we are told in Jn 3:21 and 1 Jn 1:6. And love, too, must reach into the web of everyday life, especially into that knot of small and large decisions whereby we orient our lives toward the future.

Faith consists, radically, in trying to maintain ourselves constantly before the Gospel, in which the saving will of God is revealed to us. It means accepting Christ and his teaching as they are proclaimed in the Scriptures. It is, above all, obedience to the Gospel. St. Basil said this clearly when he stated that the object of obedience is the precepts of the Gospel. St. Benedict confirmed it when he said that the function of the abbot is to explain the commandments of the Lord, that is, the Scriptures. Under this supreme norm, even on the human side, stand the rules of life (rule, constitutions or statutes). The force of the latter is rooted in their being simple applications of the Gospel. We would add that they are guaranteed by the Church. This is the ambit within which the obedience of religious is called to develop: the Gospel as applied to their own vocation. The difficulty consists in carrying this Gospel, applied by the rule, into everyday life. There are some things that offer little room for doubt. But there are many occasions when we do not know what a particular course of action may have to do with the saving will of God, so that we may well find ourselves asking, ''What relationship does this have with the love of God and his plan of salvation?''

THE PROCESS

The process through which obedience is actuated in such cases is the process of discernment. What does discerning the will of God consist in? Not in trying to verify what God has already decided. Aside from the fact that we might be playing with an all too human image of God, we could never be sure of our discernment, even in the case of a private revelation, except when something clearly contradicted the word of God. It is a matter of having to decide by ourselves, in the light of God's word, standing before his saving love. To discern the will of God means trying to see how a concrete fact may fit in with this divine love. Human responsibility—a tremendous responsibility and a great dignity—remains intact.

The first step in this process of discernment is prayer and reflection. Christians lift up their persons and lives to God in faith. They call on God for help and try to discover the direction in which the Spirit is moving them. St. Ignatius invites us to be attentive to the movements of the spirits that move or incline us toward one decision or another, and advises us to maintain an attitude of indifference toward them. Nowadays, we are also explicitly told of the need to discover the signs of the times, that is, of the events that reveal the direction in which the Spirit is moving his people. This first step can be taken either individually, when a Christian is called to make a decision on his or her own, or communitarily, when it is a community of disciples who have to make a decision. In the latter case, they pray both as a group and individually.

The second step is dialogue. Some who find it hard to move in positions of authority regard dialogue as a concession made either by authorities to subjects or by the Church to modern sensibilities. Nothing could be further from the truth. Dialogue is an integral part of the process of obedience, because nobody knows automatically, in virtue of his or her office, where the ways of God are leading. We learn to discover them, in ecclesial communion, by means of our brothers and sisters. Abbots and mothers of monasteries have always exercised their ministry as guides, in close dialogue with their monks or nuns. In matters relating to the community, their rule imposes the obligation to dialogue in important decisions. This had already been recommended by St. Basil. Dialogue is a road blocked by obstacles. Dialoguing to discern the ways of God means not going into community dialogue already knowing in advance what has to be done, or with our minds made up to impose our own will. It means listening docilely to what the others have to say and trying to put ourselves in their situation as best we can. But dialogue also means not keeping silent as a political maneuver, or because one has lost faith either in the group or in the leader. Some people isolate themselves and keep silent out of pride, others do so out of a lack of love, and not a few do so because they have already had more than their share of wounds. In reality, authentic dialogue is possible only in a community animated by mutual love.

After prayer and dialogue comes the moment of decision. One aspect of religious authority is precisely the painful responsibility of making decisions that affect others. Who must make these decisions? In a word, whoever is invested with this responsibility according to the constitutions the religious family had adopted. The Church has always recognized a twofold authority: personal authority and group authority (chapters). Theologically, this is a matter of indifference. Religious obedience is not changed because a decision is made by a person empowered to make it, or by a group. In the case of a group decision the decision may be reached either by spontaneous accord, or else by coming to a consensus that avoids extreme solutions, so that all declare their agreement with what has been decided by the group, although some might not feel personally inclined toward this solution. In cases where a consensus is not possible, the law provides for voting as an ultimate solution. This is always required in cases where the community must be juridically sure of its decision, for example in elections.

Until now, we have been speaking of obedience as a process of communion with other persons seeking the will of God who has brought us together in community. This process culminates in a decision whereby we choose what seems here and now to be most in keeping with the liberating and loving will of God. Once this decision is reached, obedience in its more limited, juridical and disciplinary sense begins. It is in this sense, says St. Thomas, that obedience arises in view of a command or a law. But it is evident, in the case of a religious community gathered together in faith and united by love, even and above all in this final phase, that obedience is much more than disciplinary or juridical matter. The community has expressed itself in a decision, and now it is up to its members to affirm their communion in faith, acknowledging this decision and carrying it out. If the community or the superior has to invoke his or her juridical authority, it is because of a failure of love.

For this very reason—because accepting and carrying out a decision is a reaffirmation of communion—individuals must set themselves, in principle, in favor of a community decision over against their own personal inclinations or opinions. For we cannot profess communion with others and then refuse to accept the consequences of this communion. It is impossible in marriage and it is impossible in religious community. The very meaning of the vow of obedience is to commit oneself to being on the side of communion and community, even against our own inclinations and judgments.

Only in serious cases (when a decision is clearly contrary to the revealed will of God or to the mission of the institute) may a religious man or woman reject the decision. There is always the danger of playing the self-appointed prophet: hence, a rejection of this sort is not legitimate, except when it comes after much prayer, reflection and consultation. Some institutes have historically come to be divided precisely because of divergent interpretations of their charism. But such divisions are always traumatic, and they can be consented to only after great efforts to maintain communion. There can be serious cases of a strictly individual character: the individual feels called to something else, or is aware before God of having ceased to be in communion of spirit with the group. In such cases, the dissent may even lead to separation. More problematic are those cases where an individual understands, before the Lord, that a decision, for example an assignment, may entail destructive consequences for himself or herself. It is hard to imagine that a superior would persist in a decision that might entail serious damage to a person. Yet it can easily happen that an individual with problems of psychological development might be overly apprehensive that something might be harmful to him or her. Some persons experience great difficulties in accepting new assignments. Nevertheless, their community or superior might judge that this change will have a renewing effect on the personality of this religious. Therefore, even in these cases, the individual must make the effort to accept the decision. Only in cases where the individual is morally certain, after consulting with experienced and prudent persons, that the decision is bound to cause him or her some harm greater than the positive value to be had by communion and obedience may the individual manifest to the superior that he or she finds it impossible to accept the decision. The superior may or may not accept this fact. In the latter case, the dissent may be so serious as to make it advisable for the individual to begin considering the possibility of separating from the institute. There are well-known cases in history, even recent history, where this process has followed the course we have described here.

The reader will note that we have been speaking only of serious cases. The reason for this, simply stated, is that it is unacceptable in principle to want to enjoy the benefits of community without also being ready to suffer for them. One cannot propose to live in communion (whether matrimonial or obediential) and at the same time decide one's present and future entirely on one's own. One cannot hope to enjoy communion and at the same time hope to live in single bliss.

Notes

1. RB 2.4; 2.11–12. RM, *ibid.*
2. RM 2.6; RM 2.6.

3. RB 3.7.

4. RB 3.3.

5. 3 Catechèse: *Oeuvres de Saint Pachôme et de ses premiers disciples,* L.Th. Lefort, ed. (Louvain, 1964) p. 45, 18–46; p. 49, 18–32.

6. *Enarr. in Ps* 99,10: PL 37,1277.

7. *Constit.* SI, 8,1.3. Cf 8,1.4; 8,1.6; 8.1,7. Letter to the Members of the Society in Portugal. Letters (Chicago: Loyola, 1959) p. 295.

8. *Int.* 13, 46, 64–65: PL 103,505–506, 514, 517–518.

9. *Req.* 1221, c. 5.

10. 2-2 q 104 a 2.

Bibliography

L. Boff, *God's Witnesses in the Heart of the World* (Chicago: CCRS, 1981) pp. 133–152.

A. Ducharme, *Spiritual Discernment and Community Deliberation* (Ottawa: Canadian Religious Conference, 1974).

J.C. Futrell, *Making an Apostolic Community of Love: The Role of the Superior According to St. Ignatius of Loyola* (Saint Louis: The Institute of Jesuit Sources, 1970).

J.M. Lozano, *Discipleship. Towards an Understanding of Religious Life* (Chicago: CCRS, 1983) pp. 227–257.

J.B. Metz, *Followers of Christ* (New York: Paulist, 1978) pp. 63–71.

F.J. Moloney, *Disciples and Prophets* (New York: Crossroad, 1981) pp. 118–129.

———, *A Life of Promise* (Wilmington: Glazier, 1984) pp. 119–163.

A. Plé, ed., *Obedience* (Westminster: Newman, 1953).

D. Rees *et al., Consider Your Call* (Kalamazoo: Cistercian, 1980) pp. 189–204.

Religious Obedience and the Exercise of Authority. Donum Dei 3. (Ottawa: Canadian Religious Conference, 1967).

J. Ridick, *Treasures in Earthen Vessels: The Vows* (New York: Alba House, 1984) pp. 85–150.

B. Rueda, *Obedience* (Ottawa: Canadian Religious Conference, 1977).

The Theology of Obedience. The Way Supplement 5. February 1968.

XI | Variety of Forms

As we moved on from the themes of celibacy and poverty to those of community and obedience, we noted at once that we had crossed a line of demarcation. In fact, the first anchorites neither lived in community nor considered community to be a value (quite the contrary). In our own times, community is not part of the life-plan adopted by hermits (even as recognized in the new Latin Code of Canon Law), nor do members of Secular Institutes make a commitment to community life. As for obedience, it was not a permanent element in the anchoritic vocation, but only a transitory phase in formation. If today's Latin Code requires even hermits to make a commitment of obedience, this is due simply to the long theological and canonical tradition developed by the cenobites, and its theological justification lies in the fact that even solitaries must maintain communion with the Church's ministers (hence, their vow of obedience to the bishop). But it is clear that a solitary's concrete experience of obedience is something quite different from that of a religious living in community.

In our reflections on the constitutive elements of the religious life, we already noticed a few differences that distinguish its various forms. We discovered, for example, two fundamental traditions concerning obedience (obedience as docility in faith, and obedience as fraternal love), and at least four forms of poverty (eremitical, cenobitical, mendicant and apostolic). Community life, for those who profess it, has taken three fundamental forms (monastic, conventual and apostolic). Note that we are referring only to basic forms; the spectrum of nuances is very broad and rich. Perhaps, before bringing our reflections to a close, we should focus on this most ample variety which the religious life has manifested throughout its historical development. If we add to this the kind of life proper to secular institutes, which shares with it some common traits, the variety of forms to be considered is still richer.

Reactions to the preliminary drafts of the new Code, especially in their attempts at describing and organizing the various forms of the religious life, made it abundantly clear how hard it is to reduce the latter to an orderly outline. Admittedly, it would be very hard to come up with a list of divisions and subdivisions in which each of the Church's many institutes would agree that they fit adequately. The phenomenon to be categorized is part of the ebb and flow of life itself, not just some well-thought-out abstraction. On a deeper level, what confronts us is the mystery of the vitality and creativity of the Holy Spirit. Nevertheless, we believe that some sort of working classification can be worked out, albeit on a rather fundamental level.

Historically, we can discover four successive forms of life committed exclusively to what the Christian people have come to call *the service of God*. First to appear was the eremitical life, characterized by total solitude. Then came cenobitism, a life characterized by separation from the world and submission to the spiritual teaching of a spiritual father or mother. Both forms of life, the eremitical and the cenobitical, came to be included under the term monachate or monasticism, for the simple reason that the cenobites had adopted so many of the ideals and, above all, the theological horizons of the hermits that they chose to be called monks (i.e., solitaries), despite the fact that they themselves professed community life. Then, in the thirteenth century, there arose what we may call the conventual life: a type of existence which, while maintaining open relationships with civil society, combined a community life (somewhat less structured than that of monasticism) with ministries. In the sixteenth century, the religious life began to be centered on apostolic or charitable activity, and ministry became the typical kind of divine service to which religious devoted the greater part of their time and energies. Finally, the twentieth century has seen the rise of secular institutes, whose members do not profess community life, but, rather, are fully integrated into civil society.

In reality, however, this distinction into successive historical phases, according to the times when different institutes were founded, although it does reveal the larger outline of an evolution, fails to mention a number of singular facts and cases. For example, it does not do justice to the fundamental difference which exists between a *generic* line of the monachate, which understands the latter as a way of life open to many possibilities of presence and ministerial activity, and a *specifically contemplative* line, which centers the monastic life' on community prayer and personal development in solitude and silence. Nor does it reveal the fundamental distinction within the mendicant group, despite the fact that all mendicants have come to embrace the conventual life. Moreover, it does not show us the notable concrete differences that exist among the institutes founded for apostolic or charitable works, which go all the way from those of a purely apostolic type (the Society of Jesus) to others in which community life plays a more demanding role (a number of Institutes) or in which withdrawal, penance, community life and the apostolate are joined in a distinctive synthesis (the Passionists). The gamut is richly varied.

Perhaps the broadest and sturdiest criterion which both embraces the various forms of life committed to divine service and at the same time reveals their distinctive differences is the one that focuses on the fundamental orientation of their very existence. There are some vocations or institutes whose whole reason for being lies in helping their followers simply to develop a type of existence that is exclusively and publicly oriented toward God and is faithful to his Gospel. And there are other vocations and institutes that orient the lives of their members toward a particular activity, thus specifying them.

If we were to apply this criterion rigorously, we would find that there are two fundamental kinds of life publicly consecrated to the service of God. One form would include an interpretation of the cenobitical monachate that considers the monachate simply as a life, yet a life that is open to the possibility of certain ministries, along with the way in which Francis of Assisi understood the religious life and as, after him, Canon Voillaume and Madeleine de Jésus have understood it, under the inspiration of Charles de Foucauld. Numerous monastic congregations, the Friars Minor, and the Little Brothers and Sisters of Jesus would come under this heading. Under the other heading would come those forms of religious life characterized by the orientation of the whole life of their members toward an activity. Some of these are oriented toward liturgical and personal prayer and form what has come to be called the contemplative life. Here we would find, on the one hand, the eremitical life, together with particular cenobitical monastic traditions, such as the Cistercians and above all the Trappists, as well as institutes like the Reformed Carmelites, whose origins reach back to the eremitical life, yet ended up adopting the conventual life that was predominant in the period during which Carmel reached its highest development. Others are oriented toward apostolic or charitable ministries (apostolic life) or join it with certain structures derived from monasticism (conventual life).

But even this framework is not without difficulties. For example, both the monachate understood in the broad sense, as an evangelical life lived in celibacy, and also the monachate understood as a life oriented toward prayer, to the exclusion of other elements of Christian life, share a very rich substrate in common, which makes any neat separation between them impossible, despite their obvious differences. Turning to another area, ministerial pressures on institutes that were originally conventual are such that the differences between them and later institutes founded specifically for ministries have dwindled significantly in the concrete practice of several local communities, although the differences in orientation and attitudes between the two types of institutes nearly always remain apparent.

All of this (such is the logic of life!) prevents us from locking into a systematization based on abstract logic. We are going to deal successively with institutes of *life* (cenobitical monasticism, groups of brothers and sisters of St. Basil and St. Macrina, Friars Minor, Little Brothers and Sisters of Jesus) and of vocations or institutes oriented toward a specific *activity:* the eremitical life, the non-eremitical contemplative life, the apostolic life in religious institutes, and secular institutes. We are fully aware that some of these forms overlap: the eremitical life is certainly contemplative, but is characterized by radical solitude; the contemplative life can be followed in monastic institutions; secular institutes are not necessarily apostolic. But within the scope of this distinction, which aims at including the distinctive traits of the various forms, each institute has its place, although it may be in tandem with two or more others: for example, contemplative monasticism and eremitism within one and the same institutions (the Carthusians and the Camaldolese), etc.

THE MONASTIC LIFE

It is not surprising that the monastic vocation and life have been given and are still being given a variety of interpretations, sometimes even by monks and nuns of the same group. The reason for this is that the Christian monachate is simply the form of religious life that appeared and developed in the Church of the Fathers within their theological horizons, both spiritual and cultural. It continued as the only form of religious life during the High Middle Ages, achieved new splendor and took on different nuances during the reforms of the eleventh and twelfth centuries, and has continued to our own times in quite different ambiences. If we adopt this definition of monasticism (the religious life that arose in the Church of the Fathers), not only are its anchoretic and cenobitic forms expressions of the same tradition, but the initiatives of Basil and Macrina, on the one hand, and of Augustine, on the other, are just as monastic as the life of the desert solitaries, the Palestinian Lavra, Syrian asceticism, the world view of Cassian and the organization of Benedict.

Nevertheless, anyone familiar both with the distinctive origins of the Basilian movement and the ideals of Augustine will be aware of profound differences between both of them and the other line of monastic life that began in the Middle East (Egypt-Palestine-Syria), spread through the West (where it was interpreted by Cassian), culminated in the rule of St. Benedict, and was enriched with fresh nuances of reinterpretation in the eleventh and twelfth centuries. The present writer prefers to relate to this tradition when he speaks of the Christian monachate, setting aside the Basilian and Augustinian movements, despite the fact that the latter share certain theological postulates and cultural conditionings with this tradition. He is not, however, unaware of the irony of the fact that the *Asketikon* of Basil (really, a catechism for an evangelical fraternity) should have become the great rule for the monachate of the Christian East. His friend, Gregory of Nazianz, informs us that Basil even intended to establish some cells for solitaries, not far from his fraternities.[1] Yet there are some distinctive aspects in this Basilian ascetical movement which its founder, after becoming a bishop, tried to draw closer to the local church. It is significant in itself that Basil avoids using the term ''monk'' in reference to his brethren (in the *Asketikon* he uses the term only once, in an almost pejorative sense) and bases his *Aske-tikon* on Scripture alone, without citing in it the points of view of the Egyptian and Palestinian ascetics whom he had visited. In his groups, the presider is not a father nor does he play a predominantly pedagogical role; community relationships are largely horizontal; the conception of obedience is different, etc. In Augustine's case, we find even greater differences, despite the fact that he frequently refers to the monks in his writings and sermons. For him, the religious life is above all a fraternal communion, his asceticism concentrates on this, his notion of obedience is (as it was for Basil) an expression of fraternal love, and the main aim he assigns to the kind of life he proposes is to revive the primitive Christian communion in the Church and before the Church. In his letter to the virgins (his *Praeceptum*), liturgical praise does not have the importance that it already had in monasticism, let alone the prominence it would receive in the rule of St. Benedict.

Leaving aside the initiatives of Basil and Augustine, we may say that monks or nuns are Christians who, following an impulse of grace, decide to dedicate their whole life to cultivating their relationship with God in celibacy and solitude, and therefore, after previously renouncing all secular goods and interests, place themselves under the direction of a spiritual master or mistress. The search for God totally defines their vocation and is the reason why they abandon human society and go into the wilderness or enter a separate community (see the explanations of cloister given by the anonymous master and by St. Benedict). Their life is above all committed to prayer (incessant prayer is the ideal) and has therefore been called the angelic life. In it, express periods of prayer alternate with periods of work, which is understood as something very human (a command of the Creator), as penance, and as a therapeutic measure. As for prayer, little by little it became organized in liturgical worship, which is carefully regulated in monasteries, becoming the starting point from which monks and nuns develop their personal prayer life. Initially, work was exclusively manual labor, but came to include intellectual work in the Middle Ages, although movements of monastic reform have continued to stress the importance of physical work.

We have spoken of "separation from the world" as a distinctive trait of the monachate, stating that it is required by the desire to commit oneself exclusively to God, trying to remain silently and peacefully in his presence. But there have been times when this separation was motivated by a negative vision of the human world. There have also been times when this separation, rather than being the result of a positive spiritual attitude, has instead been regarded as something that must be defended by strict norms and laws. Today, we still encounter a tendency toward solitude, even of the eremitical kind (and this is very much alive in certain societies), and, at the same time, a tendency to reaffirm the fact that the monastic tradition has been built up not only by separation from the world, but also by a system of fruitful spiritual and cultural relationships with the world. An interiorized monachate provides room for fruitful relationships without entailing the loss of peace and silence.

As for their spiritual horizons, the first monks seemed to have only one spiritual aim: to save their souls. They had no awareness of the fact that their vocation might have an ecclesial meaning. In order to avoid being ordained, they did not say that they were already helping the Church by their life and prayer, but simply that they could not care for others, since they were not sure of their own salvation. There was, then, a clearly individualist cast to the primitive monachate. In the Rule of St. Benedict there are indications of a greater sense of interdependence with the rest of the Church, although even here the predominant note is that of the individual's relationship with God and his vertical relationship with the abbot. The primitive monachate presented a pronounced moral and ascetical profile which is still visible in the Benedictine rule of life.[2] Nevertheless, it is already clear that Evagrius tried to raise the eyes of monks to a more mystical plane. This mystical bent developed later in the Christian East and would vigorously appear in the West throughout the twelfth century, when monks would lead their lives in the light of the Song of Songs as a loving relationship with God.

The monastic vocation expresses the very meaning of every form of religious life in its purity. For every religious life is precisely a type of existence oriented exclusively to the service of God and in relationship with the divine. Even today, monastic writers frequently tell us that the meaning of the monastic life coincides with the common Christian calling. There is something profoundly true in this (the religious life is a lived parable of the Gospel), but it should be remembered that those who claimed it during the times of the Fathers did not generally regard matrimony or secular life as a vocation, but rather as a concession to those who could not follow the vocation of virginity. From yet another point of view, if one holds a purely contemplative view of the monachate, it is hard to see how this can be identified with the vocation of disciples of Jesus, since a purely contemplative life excludes ministry, which is a typifying trait of Jesus and his Church.

FROM BASIL TO MADELEINE OF JESUS

Coinciding with this fundamental sense of the monachate as a life have been the various movements for Church reform that have given rise to religious families. These appeared for the first time with Basil and Macrina, and would reappear with Francis and Clare of Assisi. Another family that has much in common with these is the Little Brothers and Sisters of Jesus, founded by René Voillaume and Madeleine de Jésus. Both Basil and Francis aimed above all at renewing Christian life through total fidelity to the Gospel. Basil had to ascertain just what constituted the evangelical life, given, on the one hand, local reactions to the ascetical interpretation of the evangelical life brought in from Egypt and, on the other, the clerical laxity that he deplored in his writings. Francis, who was a great reforming innovator of the structures of religious life, was profoundly traditional in ordering the movement he raised up to renew that life: "This is the rule and life of the Friars Minor: to observe the holy Gospel of our Lord Jesus Christ."[3] Basil had said the same,[4] but in Francis there is a more explicitly ecclesial intention (the Church must be rebuilt). For the Poverello, it is essential that his followers offer a qualified presence before the rest of society. The Friars Minor live in the midst of the world as in their monastery. The Little Brothers and Sisters of Jesus are closer to the Friars Minor than to Basil and Macrina. For them, too, the object is a life faithful to the Gospel, but it also entails being silently present amidst the masses. Their religious life is not defined by any occupation, but by its very quality as a life. For them, any possible ministries are not institutionalized, because their proper ministry is their silent presence on the outer fringes of society.

IN THE SOLITUDE OF GOD

Over against these monastic groups, we have the much broader group of religious vocations characterized by their commitment to a determinate occupation that shapes their whole existence around it. First, however, we would like to speak of the contemplative life in its two forms, beginning with the eremitical form and then going on to those forms lived in community.

The eremitical life, in total solitude, seems to have been the primitive form of the Christian monachate, born during the last third of the third century, when ascetics who had been living in or near towns moved away from them, and, by that very fact, from the ecclesial community. Their form of life was termed angelical because, like the angels, they were always in God's presence, and also because their life was understood as a sort of return to the paradise of familiarity with God. But people were also aware that the eremitical life consisted of a constant "struggle with the demons" who dwelt in solitary places. For this reason, it came to be felt that total solitude was only for those who had arrived at a certain degree of maturity, and it eventually became a requirement that future hermits should first live under the direction of an experienced master. From this initiatory period came the notion of the *cenobium* as a school of apprenticeship, a notion that survived down to the time of St. Benedict, when the community was no longer a preparation for solitude, but a permanent vocation for some.

Those who renounce social relationships do so with a view to better cultivating their relationship with God. It is not, then, a question of psychological involution, but an attempt at immersing oneself in the divine Other. Of course, solitude, the absence of noise and words around one, can, of its very nature, facilitate the monk's encounter with self, not only in its positive aspects (one's authentic "I"), but also in its negative aspects: passions, resistances to grace, painful, tempting or dissipating memories. Hence the struggle with the demons which so many desert-dwellers experienced. But their real aim was to encounter God: not solitude in itself, but solitude as a means of a permanent encounter with God. If solitude and silence form part of the monastic vocation in general, the hermit carries them to the extreme of renouncing even the expression of community in a monastery. For this very reason, the eremitical vocation is something of an exception.

Material solitude is not enough; what is needed is interior solitude, that is, silence of spirit, in which one is progressively distanced from memories, fantasies and projects, in order to bring oneself to face the divine word. The conquest of solitude begins when the solitary is already in the desert. Saint Athanasius, in his *Life of Antony,* tells us of the temptations of remembrance that afflict beginners.[5] The hermit must divest himself of not a few concerns and memories in order to immerse himself in prayer. Immediately below, when we speak of the purely contemplative life, we shall see how the hermit comes to encounter humanity again in prayer.

The fact is, that the solitary is not just an individual, one more number in a group made up of isolated cases. As a human being, he or she is a person, that is, a consciousness which freely submerges itself in the other and, by means of this immersion of solidarity and at the same time of contraposition, affirms itself. The hermit realizes his or her personhood, ultimately, by immersing himself or herself into the divine Other who calls one and questions one. We are persons, fundamentally, before God. And it is from God that the hermit learns solidarity with his or her neighbors. The hermit is, moreover, a member of the Church. Since the Church is above all a communion in the Spirit, the hermit is doing no more than immersing himself or herself in this profound level of communion. And the Church prays in him or in her. The solitary lives, to use Peter Damian's phrase, in a *solitudo pluralis*,[6] a solitude in communion. He or she represents the Church, in adoration, somewhat in the fashion of those corporate personalities which represent Israel in the Bible.

The Christian hermit has, then, a twofold mission in the Church. In the first place, he or she enriches it with his or her experience (recall the deep influence exerted by the first anchorites) and represents it by interceding for the Church and for humanity. In the second place, the eremitical life reminds everyone not only of the uniqueness of God, but also of the transcendent value, the ineffable solitude, of the human person. It invites us to encounter both God and our own self in the depths of our being.

Men and women may lead lives deeply marked by solitude without breaking totally with their neighbors. The first fathers and mothers of the desert soon discovered the need for communication and periodically visited one another in order to seek a word of instruction. It can be most advantageous for a hermit to communicate with a spiritual director. From time to time, the hermit also needs the strengthening grace of the sacrament of reconciliation and also, in the case of an unordained person, to take part in the celebration of the Eucharist. Not even the Christian hermit is totally alone before God: he or she is also a member of the community of Jesus' disciples.

Throughout history, from the beginnings of the monachate until the present, there have been various forms of the eremitical life. There are· those who have gone into solitude on their own account, without belonging to an institution, as well as those who, with or without belonging to an institution, live with other solitaries, in order to facilitate a minimum of communication and mutual support. There are those who embrace the eremitical life after years of living in a community and remain in relationship with it, often on the grounds of the monastery. The Rule of St. Francis for hermits provides for a group of three or at most four, with one of them assigned to the service and protection of those who have chosen to embrace the solitary life. Finally, throughout the eleventh century, religious orders of hermits were founded: the Benedictine Congregations of Fonte Avellana and Camaldoli, and the Carthusians of St. Bruno. Here, the solitary life is squarely set in a broadly communitarian framework, and provides for at least a minimum of dialogue and support.

THE CONTEMPLATIVE LIFE

In speaking of solitaries, we have necessarily touched on their contemplative vocation, although we have stressed the aspect of solitude, which characterizes their life in the Church. Hence, we must now deal expressly with the contemplative life, at least in a general way, because the contemplative life is led not only by solitaries or by religious who belong to such institutions as those of the Camaldolese and the Carthusians, which were founded to facilitate the eremitical life of their members, but also in monastic orders which follow, in general, a strictly cenobitical rule (the Trappists), and in orders such as that of the Reformed Carmelites, which have deep roots in their eremitical origins and regard prayer as of the essence of the life of the institute (St. Teresa of Jesus).

We are dealing here with a type of Christian life consecrated to prayer and built around prayer as its typical trait and its distinctive form of divine service. The hermit does this in total solitude. The members of a contemplative community carry out their vocation in the bosom of a group that cultivates liturgical prayer, provides time for individual prayer and creates an atmosphere of silence and peace in order to facilitate the progressive immersion of its members in prayer. Institutes tend to promote a minimum of communication with the leader and between their brothers or sisters, in conferences, chapters and recreations. Contemplative communities usually follow a more austere rule (abstinence, fasting, poverty), aimed at keeping the spirits of their members alert for prayer.

Contemplatives take one fundamental aspect of the Christian life as the unifying element of their own life: their conscious relationship, in faith and love, with the infinite and eternal Being, the source of all, who reveals himself to us in our history and who has given himself to us definitively in Christ Jesus. This presupposes that another fundamental aspect of Christian existence—ministry—tends to be realized in the contemplative life precisely through prayer. Contemplatives serve humanity and the Church by immersing themselves in God. Hence, they renounce other active services. Any active services they may perform arise as a spontaneous overflowing of their encounter with God. Teresa of Jesus, John of the Cross, Edith Stein, Thomas Merton and even some anonymous Carthusians have addressed us on the experience of God. St. Bernard, the first Cistercians, and in our day Elizabeth of the Trinity have had a deep influence on the common spirituality of the Church. In our day, too, some Discalced Carmelite monasteries pray together with lay groups that have spontaneously grown up around them.

The whole life of contemplatives is shaped, then, by this orientation of their entire existence toward prayer. Their celibacy is a form of availability for loving encounter with the transpersonal God. Their poverty is radicalized in a spiritual sense (as in St. John of the Cross), leading them to renounce even the consolations that might come to them in prayer, so that they might seek God alone. In fact, contemplatives cannot allow either their prayer or their particular experiences in prayer to become an absolute value, taking the place of God. If they did, they would run the risk of making the latter into idols, whereupon God would deprive them of their prayer (or at least the awareness of being in prayer), their experiences, their silence and peace. The contemplative seeks God through a life centered in prayer.

A life like this reveals to the rest of the Church and to humanity the unique value of God and of the encounter with God in faith. The "God alone" of contemplative monasteries expresses precisely this meaning of the contemplative life. It is precisely in this search for encounter with God alone that the contemplative life helps the Church. Whoever enters into God by advancing into the depths of prayer (whether he or she is simply a contemplative or a mystic involved in the apostolic life) draws the whole Church in that same direction and enriches it. The difference, in the case of those who are purely contemplative, consists in the fact that this is their distinctive, vocational means of enriching the mystical body of Christ. Therefore, every mystical experience and every deepening in prayer is, of its very nature, intercession. Moreover, when they find themselves in an encounter with God alone, the disciples of the Crucified also encounter anew, on a deep level, the whole of humanity, created by God, infinitely loved by God and redeemed by God. The unique and infinite God reveals himself to us and encounters us in history. The concerns of Teresa of Jesus for the divided Church, of Thérèse of Lisieux for the missions, and of Thomas Merton for political oppression and war, all proceed from this encounter with the love and justice of God. There are times when contemplatives are called to visibly show forth the light they have received from God. According to the *Life* written by Athanasius, Antony left the wilderness to profess his faith against those who were denying the divinity of Christ. Bernard, Teresa of Jesus, John of the Cross, Thérèse of the Child Jesus, Thomas Merton and others have done so and continue doing so through their writings. Others have done so by spiritual direction in letters, such as Amparo of the Sacred Heart and Jeanne Chézard de Matel. These are all extraordinary cases of persons who have reached a high experience of the Spirit.

THE APOSTOLIC LIFE

The great majority of religious institutes founded since the sixteenth century profess an apostolic life in the modern sense of the word, that is, a life oriented toward an apostolic or charitable activity. We should recall that the expression "apostolic life" has had quite different meanings throughout history. Initially, for the anchorites, it meant imitating the apostles in their renunciation of all things. Shortly thereafter, for the cenobites, especially in the Augustinian tradition, it meant following the apostolic rule of a communion of hearts and goods. Finally, in the twelfth century, ministries were incorporated into the religious life, and in a thirteenth century document of the Order of Preachers, the apostolic life is defined as following Christ in poverty and in preaching his Gospel. In more recent times, the apostolic life has come to be understood as an existence oriented toward ministerial activities.

From the appearance of the religious life until the twelfth century, relationships between the monachate and ministry were characterized both theoretically and practically by their opposition. The anchorites withdrew from ecclesial society and the cenobites considered themselves to be a sort of incarnation of the Church, apart from the rest. The only ministries that came to form part of the monastic vocation were those directed toward the monastic community itself: spiritual guidance by the leader, sermons, etc. We know, however, that in the Middle Ages there were some outstanding missionary monks. But they were exceptions. It was in the twelfth century that religious life and ministry began to be combined systematically and doctrinally. The canons regular were clerics, who were by that very fact committed to what were then understood as ministries. Their institutions were not created for ministry, but in order to assure a life in communion, and it was from this communion that their ministerial activities flowed. Some of the hospitaller orders that arose at this time took their point of departure from this Augustinian-inspired tradition.

The first institutes expressly founded for ministries appeared in the twelfth century. First came the hospitaller orders and then, toward the end of the century, the Order of the Most Holy Trinity for the ransom of captives. Toward the beginning of the thirteenth century, the Order of Preachers was founded for the preaching of the Gospel. Shortly thereafter, the Mercedarians followed the path marked out by the Trinitarians. This time, too, saw the rise of the conventual life, in which a community life less structured than that of the monachate was joined with ministerial activities. The Dominicans created the custom of the *dispensa,* according to which a friar sent out on ministry was dispensed from community observances during the time he was working in the Lord's vineyard. However, the *observances* themselves (choral recitation of the Office, meetings, meals in common) remained intact. Parallel to this, from the twelfth century onward (Anselm of Havelberg), theologians began working out the theory of the *mixed life,* understood as an alternation of contemplation and action, with the latter derived from the former. This theory, as proposed by St. Thomas Aquinas, served as the basis for the conventual life.

The decisive step in the creation of the apostolic life as we understand it today was taken by St. Ignatius Loyola when he founded the Company of Jesus. The company was founded in order "to help souls."

Although the service of God also has a broader meaning for the Jesuits, it is embodied in ministry, because their whole life is oriented toward it, in obedience to the will of God. In an apostolic institute, everything comes to be unified around ministry. Its center is outside itself: in the rest of the Church and of humankind. The community is centered around communion in vocation and spirit, and relations of companionship and collaboration in the mission of the institute, either by working together with others in common ministries or by exercising a personal ministry as a member of the institute. Community life is much more flexible, and in pure cases, such as that of the Jesuits, it becomes totally subservient to the demands of the ministry, doing away with every act that might be an obstacle to apostolic availability. For this reason, and in order to facilitate an interior life in the midst of an often secular environment, prayer life as described in the constitutions is restricted exclusively to mental prayer. In numerous communities, almost all, in fact, a minimum of community prayer forms part of the life of the religious.

These institutes arise in order to attend to some need of the Church and of society. This need is the first thing that appears in the mind of the founder or foundress. They respond to this need through a personal ministry and therefore associate others with themselves, thus giving rise to the founding community. Therefore it is not surprising that this distinctive ministry should constitute the source of inspiration for the spirituality of the apostolic family and the criterion shaping its governance and formation.

They are religious because, like monks and members of contemplative institutes, they have utterly committed their lives and persons to the service of God in celibacy, poverty and community obedience. But they are members of apostolic institutes because, in obedience to a calling, their persons and lives are totally oriented toward the fulfillment of an apostolic mission. Their *opus Dei,* the task that has been entrusted to them by God, is their ministry. Hence, their celibacy has an apostolic meaning (as it did for Paul: to be free to attend to the affairs of the Lord), their poverty extends to the field of their ministry, and their community obedience is centered on mission.

Founded for the Church and for society, apostolic institutes have a fundamental relationship to the world of the sons and daughters of God. In virtue of their founding charism, these institutes are called to make themselves present in the world. What distinguishes them is no longer "separation from the world," but a qualified presence in the midst of society. To be sure, celibacy relates them to the kingdom of God in a way transcending natural values (this is also true of some secular institutes) and their profession of community sets them visibly before the world as religious and ministers. But the community itself is established as part of the secular city and in symbiosis with it. Apostolic religious live in a state of alertness to the needs of their neighbors and therefore to the continual flow of history.

Like the life of every Christian, the life of an apostolic religious is called to be open to the in-breaking experience of God (infused contemplation). The minister stands before his or her neighbor in an attitude of faith, both liturgical and contemplative, and accepts all the sacrifices that his or her vocation may entail. God shines through to them behind his people, and the image of Christ is visible to them in all the needy. Apostolic religious are, then, in this sense "contemplatives in action." Ministry and prayer tend to fuse together in the sense that prayer becomes intercession, and ministry lived in faith and love leads to union with God. Bear in mind that mystical experience is not the automatic fruit of long periods devoted to inwardness, nor is it the result of practicing certain psychological techniques. Mystical experience is caused by the gifts of the Spirit, and these, normally, flourish according to a greater or lesser increase in faith, hope and charity. Ministry actualizes the theological virtues and is a factor in spiritual progress. One sees God in the measure that one feels loved by him and loves him in return.

Little by little, the minister experiences a certain passivity: it is Christ the Savior who evangelizes and cares for others through him or her. St. Vincent de Paul touched on the very basis of apostolic mysticism when he recommended that his men be "passive in action." The grace that passes through a minister often arouses a surprising experience of God. At such times, we find ourselves in the presence of a mystical apostle or, to us a traditional term, a mystic in action.

Notes

1. Or. 43, 62: PG 36,577.
2. RB 4–7.
3. Reg. 1223, c. 1.

4. Int. 13, 46, 64–65:PL 103, 505–506, 514, 517–518.
5. VA 5.
6. *Liber qui dicitur Dominus Vobiscum:* PL 145,327–364.

Bibliography

T.M. Gannon and G.W. Traub, *The Desert and the City: An Interpretation of Christian Spirituality* (London: Macmillan, 1969) pp. 17–80 (monasticism), 81–114 (mendicants), 152–172 (apostolic-Jesuit).

L.M. Orsy, *Open to the Spirit* (Denville: Dimension Books, 1968) pp. 273–286.

R. McGoldrick and C.J. Yuhaus, *Facets of the Future: Religious Life USA* (Washington: Cara, 1976) (women religious).

Index of Names
(Persons, Institutions, Movements)

Theissen, Gerd, 34–35
Thérèse of Lisieux, 61, 114, 185
Third Orders, 15, 44, 67
Thomas Aquinas, 3, 9, 13, 44–45,
    96, 100, 102, 106, 120, 126,
    153, 154, 170, 186
Thomas of Celano, 41, 64
Trappistines, 6
Trappists, 176, 183
Trinitarians, 4, 5, 81, 95, 96, 99,
    130, 186

Urban II, 43
Urs von Balthasar, Hans, 87

Vincent de Paul, 5, 16, 165, 188
Vincentians, 81
Voillaume, René, 175, 180

Ward, Mary, 5, 64, 79, 145
Women martyrs of El Salvador, 78

Index Of Forms of Religious Life and Groups of Orders